Stories at Work

Stories at Work

Using Stories to Improve
Communication and Build Relationships

Terrence L. Gargiulo

PRAEGER

Westport, Connecticut
London

Library of Congress Cataloging-in-Publication Data

Gargiulo, Terrence L., 1968–
    Stories at work : using stories to improve communication and build relationships / by
Terrence L. Gargiulo.
        p. cm.
    Includes index.
    ISBN 0–275–98731–0
    1. Communication in organizations. 2. Organizational learning. 3. Storytelling—
Social aspects. 4. Storytelling—Psychological aspects. I. Title.
HD30.3.G36 2006
658.4′5—dc22   2006002745

British Library Cataloguing in Publication Data is available.

Library of Congress Catalog Card Number: 2006002745

ISBN: 0–275–98731–0

First published in 2006

Praeger Publishers, 88 Post Road West, Westport, CT 06881
An imprint of Greenwood Publishing Group, Inc.
www.praeger.com

Printed in the United States of America

The paper used in this book complies with the
Permanent Paper Standard issued by the National
Information Standards Organization (Z39.48–1984).

10 9 8 7 6 5 4 3 2 1

To "mio padre e mio maestro"
for instilling in me a passion for communication
and to Luis Yglesias
for opening my eyes to the magic of stories.

Contents

Preface

I FEEL PRIVILEGED and delighted to share my passion with you. I am an insatiable student of communication. As a child, I marveled at my father's facility as a conductor to communicate complex emotions with the twist of his baton and the sparkle of his eyes. My mother mesmerized me with her artistic interpretative power as a singer and her ability to transfer the heartfelt life she breathed into lyrics to anyone singing with her. Then as a boy soprano I had the opportunity to experience the power of story when I played the role of the crippled boy in Gian Carlo Menotti's opera *Amahl and the Night Visitors.* Every night I performed the opera, I felt an indescribable surge of electricity when Amahl is healed in the story. That experience has stayed with me until today and is responsible for inspiring the opera my father and I recently completed called *Tryillias.* These are just a few of the earliest unknowing steps I took toward understanding how we communicate deeply with ourselves and others. As with any gift, we grow into it as it patiently waits for us to catch up so it can fill us with new wonder.

It's an exciting time in the world of communication, management, and leadership. Scores of bright and dedicated thinkers, writers, scholars, and activists have added some amazing insights to our collective knowledge. Stories have a common place of prominence in all of these converging lines of thought, which include the early work in new facilitation techniques pioneered by Harris Owen, David Cooperrider's work in appreciative inquiry, Eteinne Wenger's work with communities of practices, the social capital movement, Peter Senge's work on organizational learning, Humberto Maturana and David Bohm's work on conversations, Juanita Brown and David Isaacs work with World Cafés, Noel Tichy's work in leadership,

David Boje's work on stories and countless other dedicated people too numerous to mention but all deserving acknowledgment and thanks.

I hope you make this journey they have started for us your own by bringing stories to the center of your consciousness. Give this globally expanding consciousness your own shape and shade of meaning, and, whatever you do, don't hold onto to it. Pass it along to the next eager ear and watch it catch fire in the imagination of others. Thank you for joining me, and be sure to write to me so I can learn from you. I will leave with you a story benediction I wrote:

May stories . . .
Stir your heart,
Inform your thoughts,
and Guide your actions

Warmly,
Terrence L. Gargiulo

Acknowledgments

SO MANY WONDERFUL people have fueled my passion for communication, reflection, and learning. My father has inspired me every step of the way through his genius in music. Luis Yglesias introduced to me to the uncharted waters of stories and taught me how to sail. I am forever indebted to my mother for showing me the art of care, attention, and soulful listening. I am invigorated by my sister Franca's constant encouragement to pursue my dreams. My wife Cindy's gentle spirit and generous heart knows all the ups and downs of my creative process, and I am forever indebted to her for her tireless love and belief in me. My son, Gabriel, and my daughter, Sophia Rose, are beacons of lights on my path. I hope they take any merits of my thoughts beyond my wildest imaginations. I am indebted to Eric Valentine, who has believed in my voice as an author and has taken time to help me grow and mature as a writer. Nick Philipson is awesome. He was always ready to dive into one of my wild enthusiastic brainstorm sessions with reckless abandon. He was instrumental in helping me focus and clarify my ideas. Last, I want to thank the gang at Praeger, who have been great—it's been a pleasure to work with them.

Introduction

STORIES ARE ALL around us. I am going to ask you to take a marvelous journey with me, but before we start, you must leave behind any preconceived ideas you may have about what a story is.

I'll never forget one of my first classes at Brandeis University. One of the requirements was a two-semester humanities class. I must confess I was less than excited about the class and thought it was going to be a waste of time. Nothing could have been further from the truth.

I ended up in a class taught by Professor Luis Yglesias titled "Imagining Who We Are." Professor Yglesias began by reading aloud Shel Silverstein's story, *The Giving Tree*. It's a simple story about a boy and a tree growing up together. The tree is always there for the boy. In the end, the tree gives its life so the boy can build a home for himself with its wood.

As he finished reading the story, the entire class sighed sentimentally. But Professor Yglesias did not stop. He returned to the first page of the story and reread it to us. Without editorializing, using only his mischievous eyes and the nuances of his voice, he brought the story alive in a completely different way.

Imagine our surprise when we realized that *The Giving Tree* was not necessarily a sweet story. The boy could as easily be seen as narcissistic and exploitive; the tree knew how to give, but the boy only took.

The same story that had greatly moved the class was now responsible for catalyzing emotions of outrage and disbelief. Some of us were angry for having our idealized vision of the boy and the tree shattered; some of us were incensed by the social message of selfishness and the abuse of nature implied by the story.

Professor Yglesias was not making a political comment. Nor was he trying to espouse postmodern assertions of relativism. He was simply giving us a wake-up call, and he was activating our imaginations. He was guiding us to actively connect to the story, and he was asking us to challenge our habitual response to a story we had heard many times. We were being led to discover the heart of what stories are all about. My life has not been the same since that day.

You see, stories do not fit into neat cubbyholes of meaning. Stories are a tool for reflection and insight. Stories graciously offer us the opportunity to look at ourselves and the world around us in new ways.

Stories are fundamental to the way we communicate and learn. They are the most efficient way of storing, retrieving, and conveying information. Since story hearing requires active participation by the listener, stories are the most profoundly social form of human interaction and communication.

This book will show you how to put stories to work to improve communications and build relationships. The first part of the book highlights three areas in which stories play a vital role: communicating, managing, and leading. Each area builds upon the preceding area(s). We cannot speak about management without understanding the role of communication. Stories offer us important insights into the nature of communication. Managers who strive to develop story skills will build strong relationships that are the hallmarks of an exceptional leader.

STRUCTURE OF THE BOOK

Part I, "What Stories Can Do," is divided into seven chapters. Chapter 1 examines three functions of stories central to communication: stories empower a speaker and create an environment, stories encode information, and stories are a tool for thinking. This chapter sets the stage and encourages readers to think beyond the obvious things we assume about stories. A major purpose of this book is to shift our attention away from telling stories and toward the internal and subtle underpinnings of stories. Chapters 1, 3, and 5 use ministories labeled as "vignettes" to illustrate the story functions. The vignettes come in a variety of styles and lengths. After each vignette, a few questions are posed to stimulate your own reflections. To get the most out of these vignettes, I invite you to interact with the vignettes by using your imagination, reflecting on the questions, and comparing them with your own experiences. By doing so, you will be sure to get the most of the reading and prevent the text from being didactic. I will measure the success of this book not on whether you like it, but by the extent to which readers are able to take the ideas in the book and make them their own. In this way, the book's ideas will truly have a chance to influence new behaviors that will inevitably improve communications and relationships.

Chapter 2 is a case study of the Kinship Center. The case study highlights the ways in which this organization has been successful in using stories to improve its communications.

Chapter 3 examines two more functions of stories associated with management: stories require active listening, and stories help us negotiate our differences. Active listening is at the heart of stories. If you get nothing else out of this book, make a commitment to:

Elicit other people's stories and your own, actively listen to them, and you will improve communications and build satisfying, productive, rewarding relationships in all areas of your life.

Chapter 4 is a case study of Sodexho. The case study shows how one company is trying to transform its management culture through stories.

Chapter 5 explores the qualities of leadership. Relationships are shown to be the most important work of any leader. This chapter looks at the association between awareness of self, awareness of others, and stories. Three functions of stories are discussed to understand this association: stories help people to bond with one another, stories can be used as weapons, and stories can be used for healing.

Chapter 6 is a case study of Environment for Organizational Improvement (E.O.I.), a special place where stories are used to develop new leaders. The case study looks at how one person's awareness of himself and others enabled him to take his experiences and build E.O.I., where organizations and their people can embark upon a similar path.

The three chapters in Part II, "Putting Stories to Work," offer processes, tools, and exercises for using stories to improve your communications and build relationships. Chapter 7 guides readers through a series of personal reflections aimed at developing a large collection of personal stories.

Chapter 8 shows you how to find the connections between your stories. The importance of indexing is explained. A technique I developed called Story Collaging is offered as a valuable tool for creating a strong index for putting stories to work.

Chapter 9 has a collection of exercises. The chapter is divided into two sections. The first section contains guidelines and identifies practice opportunities on how to develop keener observational skills in organizations through stories. The second section of the chapter lays out nine exercises that can be used in any type of workshop or meeting to help participants develop stronger story skills.

A STORY TO BEGIN OUR JOURNEY

Before diving into the book, let me offer you a diversion. This is Professor Luis Yglesias's favorite story. Reading it does not do the story justice, but in honor of him and his tremendous gifts as a teacher and sometimes trickster, I leave you with the story of Lady Truth:

Thomas had done it all. At the age of 50 he had become CEO of a Fortune 100 company; he had a beautiful family and all of the material things he could ever want. However, there was a gnawing question in Thomas's mind. He remembered as a young boy listening to a gospel story about Jesus. In the story, Jesus is asked, "What is Truth?" Thomas had always wondered why Jesus never replied. So one day, Thomas turned to his wife and said, "Honey, I am so happy. Our life is wonderful. But I need to go on a quest for Truth."

"Well, honey," she replied, "if it is important to you, I think you should go. I'll pack you a nice lunch, and you can give me power of attorney, and then you can head out tomorrow morning."

The next morning, Thomas took his lunch and hit the road. He left his BMW in the garage; somehow he thought he should conduct his pilgrimage on foot. So Thomas walked and walked. He stopped at his company's manufacturing plant. He had heard that workers hold the keys to Truth but he found no Truth there. Next he went to the White House. He found a lot of hot air but no Truth. Then he stopped at the Vatican to speak with the Pope, but again he found no Truth. On and on he wandered, until he found himself in a very remote part of the world. At long last he saw a sign with an arrow pointing up a hill. The sign read, "Truth This Way."

Thomas stumbled up the hill and came to a little shack with a blinking marquee, "The Truth Lives Here." He nervously knocked on the door. A moment later the door began to creak open. Thomas craned his neck around the corner to get his first glimpse of Truth. What he saw made him jump back five feet. Standing before him was the oldest, most hideous creature he had ever seen. It was all hunched over. In a high-pitched, cackling voice, it said, "Yes, dear?"

"Oh, I am terribly sorry, I think I have the wrong house. I was looking for Truth."

The creature smiled and said, "Well, you've found me. Please come inside."

So Thomas went inside and began to learn about Truth. For years Thomas stayed by the creature's side, absorbing all of the intricacies of Truth. He was amazed at the things he learned. Then one day he turned to it and said, "Truth, I have learned so much from you, but now I must go home and share my wisdom and knowledge with others. I do not know where to begin. What should I tell people?"

The hideous old creature leaned forward and said, "Well, dear, tell them I am young and beautiful."

In the words of Mark Twain, "Sometimes you have to lie a little bit to tell the truth."

Part I / *What Stories Can Do*

1 / *Communicating through Stories*

EFFECTIVE COMMUNICATION DEPENDS on stories. This chapter explores three functions of stories that facilitate communication. To begin with, stories empower a speaker and help him or her create an environment. This is one of the more obvious uses of stories in communication. Most of us recognize that we are more persuasive when we use a story to transmit ideas. Instead of telling someone what we mean, we use stories to show them what we mean. As a result, people are more engaged and receptive to what we are communicating. The second function explains how stories encode information. The cliché, "What's the moral of the story?" characterizes how stories are used as containers for values and other types of information. Although stories can be used to broadcast predigested messages, the range and impact of such broadcasts is often overestimated. We will touch upon this theme shortly. The last function examines how stories are a tool for thinking. We cannot divorce our thinking from our communications. Because stories encode information, we can manipulate large chunks of concepts and ideas. The quality of what we communicate is directly tied to our thinking.

STORIES EMPOWER A SPEAKER AND CREATE AN ENVIRONMENT

Let's begin our discussion by exploring some of the ways stories empower a speaker and create an environment. How do you grab someone's attention? It seems to be getting harder and harder to be heard. Ironically, the glut of information at our disposal has hindered rather than helped the quality of our communications. Whether in written or verbal form, stories empower a speaker. Think of the story as a certificate of authenticity. When we use a story, we are offering listeners our credentials. It is as if we are saying, "Direct your attention this way—I have something you want to hear." Speakers are empowered when listeners give them their attention. Once a social contract has been made between a speaker and listeners, the speaker can use his or her sphere of influence to create an environment. The speaker's purpose could be anything from entertaining to relaxing, engaging, teaching, reflecting, or stimulating dialogue.

Facts have a short shelf life. Try this thought experiment: on a piece of paper write down as many facts as you can remember about one of your parents in one minute. How long is your list? It's probably not very long. Granted, if you had more than a minute, it might be longer. However, our minds do not work in terms of facts. Did any of the facts trigger the memory of a story? Or did one story lead you to another one? Some memory experts contend that the average person can hold about seven to nine items in short-term memory. Where does all of our information go? Lists fall short because they lack the richness found in stories. If our minds do not work in terms of facts, it stands to reason that facts are also not the best communication vehicles.

Stories blaze the trail for our communications. Think of stories as allowing communicators to prepare the proverbial soil for whatever ideas or information they want to plant. The story operates like the seed of a plant, burrowing its roots in the minds of listeners who associate themselves with the story by activating their experiences. A communicator then can harvest the fruits of these efforts. It is not the clarity of communication that empowers a speaker but the richness of the communication. And the richness comes from a story's ability to tap into listeners' experiences. If a speaker uses a story to empower listeners, the speaker also becomes empowered. We have to make a distinction between "wowing" an audience and reaching an audience. Wowing an audience may feel empowering but does not necessarily provide an enriching or learning experience for listeners. People are easily dazzled by appearance and sound. Stories can be used for more than grabbing people's attention. Stories are vehicles for learning when they provide a way for people to connect their experiences to the teller's story. True communication works at building and sustaining relationships. Stories connect us to others—they serve as bridges between our experiences and the experiences of others.

Vignette #1: Shazam

Jack approached the podium with confidence. He could not believe it had been over 20 years since his high school graduation. The perfunctory applause died down, and Jack's eyes met the stares of over 500 students and their parents awaiting his words of wisdom.

Jack took a beat of silence and then raised his fist in the air and yelled, "Shazam!" into the microphone. Without waiting for his startled audience to settle back in their seats, Jack continued.

"Ms. Picasso was her name. Paints, charcoal, and papier-mâché were the game. Room 62, second period, on Mondays and Thursdays, this was my junior year nightmare. I must have flunked preschool, because to this day I cannot draw a circle and color it yellow inside. To avoid sinking into a pool of artistic self-contempt, I used art class as an opportunity to religiously pursue one of my favorite subjects: flirting! Ms. Picasso and I had very different agendas. She could not understand how anyone could resist being drawn into her world of shapes, colors, and perspectives. I could not understand why she insisted on trying to sell us on her passion, even as she persisted in interfering with mine.

"Art was her strength, and discipline was her weakness. Whenever our class got out of control, Ms. Picasso would yell '!' Perhaps some of you have seen a TV show called 'The Greatest American Hero.' The main character was your typical nerd by day, superhero by night. Whenever he had to transform himself from nerd to superhero, he would yell his magic word. And what word do you think he yelled?"

Questions for Reflection

Before reading any further, take a few moments to think about the following questions:

1. Do you see more than one story here?
2. What are the potential effects on the audience of the stories Jack uses?
3. How does the word "Shazam" function in the story?
4. Try to imagine some of the ways Jack might incorporate these stories in the rest of his talk.

Analysis

Every speaker faces the challenge of engaging an audience. Try to recall the most memorable speakers you have heard. Undoubtedly, you are recalling a story or anecdote the speaker used to anchor the talk. Jack remembers what it was like to be a high school student. Jack's story is funny. We are drawn into the picture he paints of art class with his idiosyncratic art teacher. However, there is more than humor in this story. If Jack is merely an accomplished public speaker with all of the skills and techniques of the trade, he may not realize how he can use his story to reach deep into the minds of his audience and not just entertain them.

In a short introduction to his talk, Jack weaves two stories together. The main story of Jack's art teacher is dependent upon his reference to *The Greatest American Hero* TV show. For some listeners, "Shazam" will be enough to elicit their index of the superhero story, but for those who are not familiar with it, Jack quickly gets them up to speed. This is one of the important aspects of stories that are over-looked. Stories do not need to be long. Single words can act as stories if people share the same word as an index of the story. Connecting stories to one another is a powerful tool for speakers and anyone interested in catalyzing people's imaginations.

Jack's story allows him to be vulnerable in front of his audience. His talk is to a group of high school students about to take a ceremonial step toward adulthood. Memories of failing art and goofing off in a class taught by a quirky but passionate teacher, reviewed later in life, can yield rich lessons. Jack can now weave a collage of stories and anecdotes that chronicle his maturation. Stories and experiences must be seen in relation to one another. Stories in isolation are deprived of their fullest potential.

DISCUSSION STORIES ENCODE INFORMATION

Stories are the best way to encode information. Complex information can be stuffed into succinct, easy-to-digest packages. Listeners can unwrap the story's packaging and uncover a wealth of information in the process. People are quick to equate stories with morals. Although it is certainly true that one of the many forms of stories (i.e., fables, tales, allegories, etc.) can be used to carry value-laden messages, this is not the full extent of how stories can encode information. Stories are full of information hidden from our immediate perspective. Likewise, the listener as well as the teller is impacted by encoded information in a story. A listener may decode information presumed not to be present or intended by the teller. Through personal associations, the listener of a story is apt to discover new insights. The teller is not the only one responsible for the information passed on in a story. How a listener decodes a message is an important facet of generating meaning.

Here is another way of thinking about the way in which stories encode information. Stories are like holograms. Holograms are special three-dimensional pictures produced with an interference pattern of laser beams. Holograms are unique because of the multiple perspectives contained in the pictures and because a single pixel of a hologram contains all the information for the entire picture. Like holograms, stories are packed with information and interfacing possibilities. These interfacing possibilities are the ways in which a story can be connected to another one. Stories in isolation are of little communication value; however, stories reflectively arrayed in a mosaic offer a host of learning opportunities. In this way our stories lead to insights and appear to leap through rapid and often unexpected associations.

How many times have you revisited a story and learned something new in the process? Stories need to be revisited frequently in order to reap their benefits. Furthermore, stories connected to one another create new opportunities for insights. Information previously unavailable comes to the forefront. Stories work best in relation to one another. One story sheds light on the other, and through the endless possible combinations we can discover new connections between our stories. We will explore this theme in greater detail in the second half of the book when we work with story collages.

This latent ability of stories to provide ongoing information is a powerful capacity of their communication potential. The problem is that if we cannot fully control what information is decoded, we cannot manage the communication power of the stories. If we are to become effective communicators through stories, we must accept that we cannot fully control the information encoded in a story or its impact. It is neither possible nor desirable. Herein lies one of the subtlest but most important truths about stories: they are in essence governed by self-organizing principles.

Let's use an image of the brain's physiology as a visual metaphor to illustrate this principle of stories. Our brains contain complex, expansive, branching highways of networked neurons. Much is still being discovered about the nature of these networks, but researchers have observed that these networks of neurons are created and maintained on the basis of our usage of them. Unused pathways dry up like tributaries robbed of their water. Pathways with lots of traffic are strong and begin to connect themselves to other pathways to create a highway of electrical stimulus for the brain. Stories operate in much the same manner.

The underlying power of stories teeters on a dangerous precipice where purpose and randomness play a game of tug-of-war. To use a Greek word, stories are stochastic. That is, stories are not predetermined scripts that we are destined to inevitably discover once we have a life experience, nor are they completely random events devoid of any inherent meaning. Working with stories purposefully to communicate meaning to others and ourselves demands that we find a way to sit with this paradox.

Our experiences are recorded as memories in the form of stories in our minds. Stories act as subjective placeholders. In other words, every time we tell a story, we resurrect our memories. These stories usher in a host of reflective opportunities. Telling stories not only makes us more effective communicators, but also offers the gift of insight. In essence, stories enable us to communicate more effectively with ourselves. As we become more aware of our stories, we become like archaeologists forever unearthing new treasures of meaning. Being more purposeful and mindful of telling stories will inevitably lead us to new nooks and crannies of insights.

Let's try another analogy. The deoxyribonucleic acid known commonly as DNA holds all of our genetic information. Our genetic code is composed of four nucleotides, which bond in pairs and entwine themselves in a double helix strand. These four nucleotides are responsible for an incredible amount of variation. Even one alteration in a pair of nucleotides of a DNA strand can result in dramatic changes in the organisms in which they are expressed. Our experiences are like DNA, and our experiences stored as stories are like the nucleotides of the DNA molecule. Our stories are the means by which recombinant reactions cause new meaning to emerge—this is not generating meaning but rather the spontaneous phenotypic expression of something new.

STORIES ARE TOOLS FOR THINKING

We take for granted that effective communication requires clear thinking. We may feel like our mouths run on autopilot, but how do we actually determine what we are going to say to another person? Have you ever tried giving a formal presentation or writing a long document without an outline? These tasks require organization, and the complex extemporaneous communications we engage in every day are similar in this respect.

So what fuels our thoughts? Is it an abstract process left to cognitive scientists to study or is there something we can infer about what goes in our minds? Stories offer us a way of looking at the inner workings of our minds. Thoughts are by-products of our experiences. Specific experiences may not be in the forefront of our mind, but we build a perceptual filter of the world based on them. Stories support a lattice of human experiences. Each new story acts as a tendril tying us to the past, making the present significant, and giving shape to the future. In this way, a story from the past can be joined to other stories, help us establish connections with people, and inform future behavior. Stories are the language of the imagination, and our imagination speaks in stories.

Imagination is a central part of understanding effective communication. Despite our earnest efforts, we are not rational. Our decisions and behaviors are motivated by a host of irrational factors that are buried deep in a black box penetrable only through circumspection of our experiences accessed as stories. We assemble all these invisible experiences from our past to generate a rationale to explain ourselves and express our thoughts in a clear manner, but this is a facade of rationality. The irrational is tempered by the rational, and the final cognitive results are very convincing.

When we invoke our imaginations, stories become a tool for thinking. Our mind can move in two contradictory directions at the same time. A quick way to grasp this idea is to consider the odd nature of dreams. Arguably, dreams are a type of story. In a dream we can feel as though we are walking and flying at the same time, tasting what we are hearing, seeing one person but feeling like they represent two or more people, and so on—and none of this is problematic to us while we are dreaming. Stories as tools for thinking grace our waking minds with this same ability as dreams. They work with paradoxical elements without becoming derailed by the dissonant particulars. We can use our minds in nonlinear ways. Two points of view can be true. We are not compelled to rush forward in a mad march to a singular rational conclusion. Our minds can meander and discover new nuances. Through the mechanisms of stories, we can entertain another perspective without losing our own. An effective communicator is not blindsided by rational conclusions. An effective communicator may have confidence in his or perspective, and voice it with persuasive force, but with the aid of stories as a thinking tool he or she can also remain sensitive, open, and understanding of other viewpoints.

Stories equip our minds with templates for thinking. We can use stories to describe one thing in terms of another. New concepts are not abstract if we use stories or analogies that resonate with a person's knowledge and experience. For example, I remember teaching a class on technical writing. Many students struggled with writing clear and succinct explanations, so I had them take a technical concept and explain it using an analogy a teenager could understand. The hard part was thinking of an analogy or metaphor that applied to the concept. The rest was straightforward. They were amazed at how easy the concept was to explain and how simple it became once they found an analogy.

Stories are particularly effective thinking tools when the imagery is distinctive. Take the following short phrase and the story behind it: "Canary in a coal mine." The contrast of a bright yellow canary with a dark coal mine is a striking image. Coal miners used to carry a caged canary into the mines. If the canary died, they knew the air in the mine was not safe.

A leader might use the image of a canary in a coal mine with a group of managers tasked with a potentially disastrous project. Undoubtedly, the team feels uneasy. They may even believe that the business is setting them up for failure. Emotions left unexpressed can hamper objective decision-making. However, the image of the canary does not need to be negative. Story thinking enables us to validate emotions and articulate possibilities. A leader can guide his or her team from negative emotions of fear and resentment about being set up for failure to positive ones of excitement about the challenge that lies ahead of them. The story can be rewritten. Why not give the story a new spin? The canary neither has to die or be stuck in a cage. Build upon the story. Point out that, unlike canaries, the team is free to make choices to avoid disaster. Show how the team will be brave pioneers for the business.

Learning results from piecing together our experiences. One experience builds on another. We are pattern-recognition machines. Studies of chess players have shown that one of the major differences between novice and expert players is that experts, faced with a novel board position, draw upon previous games with similar positions to select the best move. Experts have more experience, and, whether they realize it or not, they apply that experience to novel situations.

I remember hearing an anecdote about a famous spiritual teacher. His students challenged him to tell them what lessons they could learn from catching a train or sending a telegram. He replied, "A train teaches us that even a second can make a difference, and a telegram teaches us to measure all of our words because every one of them counts." This demonstrates the flexibility and applicability of stories as tools for thinking and reflection. The act of catching a train or sending a telegram is not intrinsically loaded with meaning. Thinking analogically produces a unique twist.

Case studies are another example of story thinking. They are marvelous teaching tools and generate many great discussions. Case studies replace the abstractions of business theory with story. They also broaden the learning process. Previous case studies can be related to the one currently being discussed.

Stories are wonderful thinking tools. Through stories we reflect on our experiences. Experiences mean nothing if we don't learn anything from them. Stories bring the past viscerally alive to our minds. When we retell a story, our mind relives the experience. Each rewinding of our mental tape recorder is an opportunity to gain new insights.

We all have many experiences and therefore many stories. To put a twist on Plato's saying: "The unexamined story is not worth having."

Vignette #2: Precision Dynamics

Phil Anderman, president and CEO of Precision Dynamics, had no idea why his company had fallen on such bad times. Profits were down, morale was low, and interdepartmental feuds threatened to turn a bad situation worse.

Phil knew he needed to change the organization's culture. Currently, departments were competing for vital resources. The company's structure, which he had put in place, did not encourage the integration of resources. At the time, the strategy had sounded brilliant: encourage innovation and teamwork by fostering a competitive environment. Now, with the luxury of hindsight, he knew he had been wrong.

Tomorrow morning he was to meet with all the departmental heads, and he wasn't sure what he was going to say. Well, first things first, he thought. It was time to tuck his daughter into bed. Morning would come soon enough.

When Phil walked into the conference room the next day, it was buzzing with uncertainty and suspicion. There had been a lot of rumors and people were on edge; so was Phil, for that matter.

"Good morning everyone. Please take a seat so we can get started; we have a lot to discuss. Last night I sat at home agonizing about what I should say this morning. As I was tucking my 10-year-old daughter Maya into bed, she shared with me a story she had heard at school. It goes something like this.

"There once was a farmer. After working all morning in the scorching sun, he sat down under a shady tree to take a rest. Wiping the sweat from his eyes, the farmer thought, 'Oh, I wish I had some cool, clear water to splash on my face.' Suddenly a pail of water fell from the tree, drenching the farmer below.

"'That felt so good,' the farmer said to himself. 'I just wish I had some more water to quench my thirst.' This time a bucket of water appeared by his side. Now, the farmer was no dummy. He knew that he had stumbled upon a wishing tree and that he had only one wish left. Lifting his voice to the leaves above, he said, 'I want to meet the wisest teacher.'

"Before he had even completed uttering his wish, a robed figure appeared before him. He asked the farmer, 'What would you like to learn or see?'

"Without hesitation, the farmer replied, 'I want to learn how to get to heaven.'

"The teacher's sparkling blue eyes flashed, and suddenly the ground in front of the farmer opened up with a fierce rumble and an escalator leading downward appeared. The farmer asked the wise teacher, 'Where will this take us?'

"The teacher smiled and said, 'The way to heaven is through hell.'

"They both stepped onto the escalator and began their descent. At last they saw a sign that read, 'Welcome to Hell—Banquet Hall Straight Ahead.' The farmer was awfully hungry from the long trip. He turned to the teacher and said, 'Let's go get some food.'

"They headed for the banquet hall. As they entered, the farmer stopped in his tracks at the magnificent sight. There were long marble tables with large vases filled with bright and sweet-smelling flowers. Each table held dozens of gold trays heaped with the most delectable foods.

"The farmer turned to the teacher and said, 'I don't understand.'

"'Look very carefully,' responded the teacher.

"The farmer suddenly noticed food flying all over the place. People were swarming from one table to another grabbing food from golden trays. Then the farmer saw what the teacher wanted him to observe; the elbows of each person were permanently locked, so their arms remained fixed straight in front of them. People were attempting to eat the food from the trays by throwing it in the air and then trying to catch it in their mouths. As a result, food was flying everywhere and very little of it was actually getting eaten.

"In a pleading voice the farmer said, 'May we go now? I have seen enough.'

"The teacher nodded, and in the wink of an eye they were on another escalator and climbing into the sky. At long last it stopped by a sign that read, 'Welcome to Heaven—Banquet Hall Straight Ahead.'

"So the teacher and farmer went to the banquet hall, and again the farmer stopped dead in his tracks. The banquet hall was identical to the one in hell, with long, marble tables decorated with large vases filled with bright and sweet-smelling flowers and gold trays heaped with the most delectable foods.

"The teacher guided the farmer toward one of the tables. As the farmer approached he felt his elbows lock straight. Glancing around the room, he realized that everyone was in the same predicament. Even the teacher's arms could not bend. The teacher spoke: 'We are hungry. Let us eat.' With that, he picked up a piece of food and extended it toward the farmer's mouth. The farmer did likewise, and they ate to their hearts' content. When the farmer had chewed his last morsel of food, he found himself, once again, in the shade of the wishing tree.

"I'm afraid I have neither a wishing tree nor wisdom to offer you. We are going through some tough times. I realize that we have not always made the best decisions, or implemented the best policies, but I firmly believe we can get through this. Before we dive into the strategic plan, would someone please pass me the coffee?"

Questions for Reflection

1. How does Phil use his daughter's story to create an environment? In what ways does the story empower him?
2. Is there any significance to the fact that the story comes from Phil's daughter?
3. What is the relationship between the story and Phil's company?
4. What are some ways Phil's staff might react to the story?

Analysis

Phil recognizes the relevance of the story his daughter heard in school to his company's predicament. He shows us how a story or experience becomes an opportunity for reflection and insight. Phil's receptivity to the story is a defining characteristic of the "story mind"; it does not matter that the story comes from a child. The story mind develops the discipline of synthesizing information. Although on the surface there is no apparent connection, the story mind looks for relationships between ideas and concepts from different areas and experiences.

Phil decides that he does not need to put up a false front of strength and leadership in order to motivate his managers. On the surface, he risks appearing vulnerable by alluding to the ineffective policies he instated that encouraged competition between departments, by expressing his uncertainty and apprehensions about the company's present position, and by sharing a story told to him by his daughter. But that very vulnerability and use of the story creates an environment of trust. The story encapsulates the changes the company will need to embrace in order to regain market share. And deliberately or not, Phil ends his story by asking someone to pass him the coffee. To Phil, the story about getting to heaven through hell is not just an allegorical tale; it is a template for his thinking and communication.

What if Phil had said this instead: "We all know that Precision Dynamics has fallen on hard times. Sometimes a company needs to go through a little hell before it can reap the benefits of growth. Now more than ever you need to pull together as a team and do whatever it takes to beat the market's down cycle. We will not allow our competitors to push their way into our value chains. Today I will take you through our strategic plan for the next quarter. It is imperative that you follow the road map set out in this plan. Precision Dynamics' success rests in your hands."

Here Phil sounds like a no-nonsense CEO. He gets to his point quickly and tells his managers what they need to do. But is he as effective? The tone is dictatorial. When was the last time you changed your behavior because of a motivating speech? Words can be silvery; all of us can be moved by a person's charisma and rhetoric, but we rarely identify with the speaker or undergo a significant shift within ourselves. Phil's tone and words are unlikely to elicit the response he seeks. He is presenting a strategy of teamwork, but he is clearly setting himself apart from the team.

A colleague of mine was once named director of a dysfunctional department. For years people had been bickering and fighting. Over the course of a year and a half, things improved. At the department's annual holiday party, my colleague decided to tell the "The way to heaven is through hell" story and act it out with his staff assistant. The response was unbelievable. Managers came up to them after the party and said, "Thank you for showing us the way out of hell."

Vignette #3: Quality Control

Company X's first quarter results for 1999 were in, and the final numbers were staggering. Janice Shaker, president and CEO of the company, was sitting at her desk reading a slew of congratulatory e-mails from members of the board of directors when John Moore, vice president of manufacturing, came bursting into her office.

"I really don't know what to do, Janice," he began. "I have tried everything I can think of, but nothing seems to be working. For the past three months, the number of defective products shipped and returned to us has been increasing. Let me give you an idea of the scope of this problem: Last month, 20 percent of our products shipped were returned for a refund. I met with the folks in manufacturing to see if they had any ideas or required any help. They believed the root of the problem was sloppy and careless work by the team of quality control engineers.

"I met with Tim Jenkins, the director of quality control, and he assured me he would have a talk with his team of engineers. One month later, things have only gotten worse. I heard through the grapevine that Tim threatened to fire his manager of quality control if things did not improve."

Janice took a moment to think. Then she smiled to herself and said to John, "Thanks for the heads up. I'll take it from here. Oh, by the way, be sure to clear next Tuesday on your calendar for a luncheon with all of manufacturing to celebrate our record-breaking quarter."

Janice watched John walk out of her office shaking his head. She sighed to herself and closed all of the open e-mail messages from the board of directors and quickly wrote the following memo:

> FROM: Janice Shaker
>
> TO: All Employees of Manufacturing/Quality Control
>
> SUBJECT: Luncheon
>
> Our results from the last quarter are in and I am proud to inform you that all of your hard work and dedication has paid off. We exceeded everyone's expectations. I think we all deserve an opportunity to celebrate a little. On Tuesday, all manufacturing will stop at 1:00 P.M. for the day. We will have a specially catered luncheon. At 3:00 P.M., everyone will be free to go home early. I am attaching a menu; please return your selections to my office by 4:00 P.M. Friday.
>
> Looking forward to seeing and speaking with you then.

Janice called in her assistant, Chris. "Chris, would you please ask Sea Point Catering to cater a 1:00 P.M. luncheon for us on Tuesday. When you get them on the phone, please buzz me; I need to go over a few things with them."

It didn't take people long to return their menus. Everyone was eagerly awaiting delicacies like lobster Fra Diavolo, haddock stuffed with king crab legs and shrimp, and soft shell crabs, to name just a few of the selections.

At 1:15 P.M. on Tuesday, Janice walked into the reception hall. Chris and John ran up to her in a panic. John blurted, "You'd better have a word with the caterers. No one has the food they ordered. Every single order is wrong. How could these people be so incompetent?"

Janice brushed past them and walked toward the podium. She observed people frantically swapping plates in an attempt to get the dish they had ordered. Silence fell upon the room as Janice began to speak. "Good afternoon, everyone. Let's all dig in and enjoy our scrumptious lunches from Sea Point Catering." Before Janice could continue, she heard Tim Jenkins mutter, "We would if we had the food we ordered." Janice focused her eyes on Tim and slowly issued the following request, "Will Sea Point Catering please serve everyone their meal according to the second seating plan I faxed you."

In less than five minutes everyone had exactly what he or she had ordered. When Janice spoke during dessert, she thanked and congratulated everyone for all of their hard work. She shared her vision for the next quarter, emphasizing the critical role of making their customers happy by ensuring the highest-quality product. Janice concluded by apologizing on behalf of Sea Point Catering. She claimed full responsibility for the mix-up, since she had faxed them two different seating plans.

At the end of the luncheon, John walked up to Janice wearing a sheepish grin and said, "You did that on purpose, didn't you? Well, whether you did or not, Tim definitely benefited from the experience. I heard him and his manager strategizing with their team of engineers on ways to improve quality control." Janice just smiled. Maybe now she could get back to responding to some of those glowing e-mails.

Questions for Reflection

1. How do Janice's and John's responses to the quality control problem differ?

2. How are Janice's actions an example of how stories encode information?
3. Will Janice's actions have any other longer-term effects on the organization and its employees?

Analysis

Stories are efficient encoders of information. For example, in stories from different cultural, religious, or mystical traditions, lessons or meanings are never spelled out. Instead, you are invited to connect to a story or experience through active listening, to unravel the story's significance, and generate your own meaning. In this way, stories are also fluid. As you return to your stories and memories, new nuances, insights, and shades of meaning emerge.

In this story, Janice concluded that Tim's efforts to impress upon his team of engineers the impact of poor quality control and his attempts to motivate his manager with threats had been ineffectual. She realized that she had to find a more dramatic way than Tim's traditional approach to make the point. Janice decided to model the frustrating result of an experience with bad quality control by having everyone's lunch order purposely mixed up.

Experiences can be used to tell a story. Up until this point, we have examined stories as communication vehicles through the telling. In this example, Janice used her imagination to conjure up a scenario. She created the situation she needed in order to encode her message. Her story thinking led her to construct an experience that stimulated the imagination of Tim and his team. Janice, being a true leader, guided Tim toward a creative solution to the problem. He and his team are not likely to forget Sea Point Catering's luncheon. Janice not only succeeded in addressing the quality control problems, but she also created a story that will inevitably become part of the company's culture.

SUMMARY

Effective communicators use stories. Three functions of stories are central to communication. Stories empower a speaker and help him or her create an environment; stories are efficient encoders of information; and stories acts as tools for thinking. If a picture is worth a thousand words, a story must be worth a hundred thousand words. Thinking with stories enables us to process a lot of information. Lengthy and logical reasoning processes are accelerated with story thinking. The foundation of working with stories is communication with others and self.

2 / Case Study—Kinship Center

THE PREVIOUS CHAPTER detailed three functions of stories that play a central role in making us effective communicators. We explored how stories empower communicators, how they can encode information, and how they act as tools for thinking. Our next stop is to observe how one organization identified some of its key stories for communicating its mission to the outside world and helping people within the organization understand its strengths.

BACKGROUND ON THE KINSHIP CENTER

The Kinship Center is an agency dedicated to the creation, preservation, and support of foster, adoptive, and related families for children who need them. The agency's work aims to achieve and sustain permanency for children in family settings, avoiding institutional placement, and supporting children and families to grow, heal, and thrive. It was created in Monterey County in 1984, following the closure of an old statewide child placement agency. The staff who began the program remain as leaders of the agency, including the executive and assistant directors and the senior social worker. Individuals from the community's private, public, and legal sectors have loaned their time and business expertise consistently over 20 years to help this grass-roots organization achieve its current status. The agency is respected locally, regionally, and statewide and has a significant national reputation for leadership, education, and creative approaches to solving services problems in child welfare.

In 2004, more than 1,200 children statewide in California received significant services in child placement, children's mental health, and special family services such as adoptive family wraparound and relative caregiver programs. The agency's

Education Institute provided psychoeducational groups to families and clinical training to therapists and child welfare professionals statewide. More than 3,500 California therapists and social workers have taken the Kinship Center's Adoption Clinical Training classes. The Kinship Center operates the first two adoption and permanency-specialty child mental health clinics in the country that are funded by EPSDT MediCal. The two clinics currently serve more than 240 children and their families each week. The clinics have been cited as providers of promising approaches in managed care for child welfare by Georgetown University, and the center has received two national Excellence in Adoption awards from the Secretary of Health and Human Services for its support of adoptive families.

I became aware of the Kinship Center when my wife began working there as a clinical social worker in the agency's D'Arrigo Children's Clinic. A dynamic duo of Carols (Carol Bishop and Carol Biddle) blends their unique talents and passions to guide the organization. These articulate and devoted women were quick to tell me all the ways in which stories are central to their organization. Stories empower them to communicate the impact of the agency's work. People connect to the agency's mission through the stories it tells, and members of the staff maintain a sense of urgency and energy for their tireless work through the stories shared. Each story retold encodes countless others.

The stories below represent a sample of stars bright in the cultural constellation of the Kinship Center. Each story echoes one of the agency's key themes. The agency relies on these stories as tools for thinking about itself and understanding its evolving mission. Besides being touching stories, they showcase the multifaceted communication potential of stories. Beyond the compelling images portrayed in these examples, these stories also transmit key aspects of the agency's identity and act as tools for thinking.

The stories are written by Carol Biddle and other members of the agency. As much as possible, I have left the stories in their voice. Each story is followed by a brief discussion of how it relates to the three communication functions of stories discussed in chapter 2 (empowers the speaker, creates an environment, and is a tool for thinking). The discussion following each story is written by me and sometimes includes quotes from Carol Biddle highlighting how she and other members of the agency use the stories.

KINSHIP CENTER STORIES

Theme #1: Mission and Resilience

In the late 1980s, the Kinship Center had less than five years of history as a licensed agency when this crisis/opportunity presented itself.

One of those "Friday afternoons in child welfare" calls came regarding a two-year-old medically fragile child who had spent months, off and on, in a major teaching hospital. She had been alternately in foster care, with her very young single mother, and back in the hospital because of her multiple medical disabilities. When Kari was released from a regional teaching hospital, she was taken into protective custody again because her young mother could not care for her, although she tried. Kari's disabilities included an uncorrected cleft palate (severe), various congenital anomalies, and a requirement that she be fed through a tube inserted into her throat (she could not swallow).

Miraculously, there was a willing foster family, the Bakers, who had cared for children with cleft palates and those requiring feeding tubes. The county social worker carried the child into the foster home, and all present were appalled to see a two-year-old who weighed less than 12 pounds, wrapped in a receiving blanket and wearing only an infant T-shirt and diaper.

The fragile child was taken to the local hospital to be evaluated by a pediatrician. The physician and hospital staff spent several hours evaluating the child and instructing the foster mother on inserting the feeding tube successfully. Kari was discharged to the foster mother's care with appointments for regular follow-up.

Within weeks, Kari began to gain weight and settle into this unusual and dedicated family. She was scheduled for an appointment at Stanford Medical Center for evaluation and to determine the feasibility of future surgery to make her feeding easier. The foster family adored this little girl. Kari's foster mother, Diane, transported her in a front-loading infant carrier for months. Kari was initially so small and still that the carrier, under a coat, made Diane look pregnant. This tiny child gradually gained weight and became responsive. She would even occasionally smile and look into Diane's eyes. The Kinship Center staff was gratified and delighted with her care and progress.

Kari eventually had surgery, allowing her to be fed through a "G" tube in her stomach. However, a state licensing worker visited the home and declared that this child needed institutional care and would need to be moved immediately. With some feelings of distress, the dilemma was presented to the board of directors, with the Kinship Center staff recommendation that this child not be moved again because she was doing so well and because of her need to continue her healthy attachment to this family. The agency's pediatric consultant supported the staff recommendation. The board members recommended and supported a formal appeals process to the licensing agency, giving the Kinship Center a chance to keep this child safely placed in a family.

The appeals process continued for more than one year, with volumes of paperwork and the state sending consulting physicians to see the child. The net result was that Kari was allowed to stay in the foster home, but the ruling was not considered to be a precedent. The foster family adopted Kari. Ultimately, Kari died at age 12 of complications of her fragile physical state and her developmental disabilities. The actual results were much larger than extending her life and providing her with a family, although that would have been a sufficient outcome. Kari became an inspiration to her family, her church and school community, and to the staff and board at the Kinship Center. She had the highest quality of life that could be given to her, was a happy child, and shared lessons about normalizing care for developmentally disabled children to all whose lives she touched.

Beyond the happy family outcome, for the Kinship Center, the lasting lesson was discovering the courage to dissent and to challenge, at the risk of losing state licensing. When faced with adversity, the measurement of the agency's mission impelled courage, determination, and an organizational life lesson about advocacy. Kari provided an early and significant learning opportunity about claiming the stated values that were integral to the mission of the organization.

Discussion

This moving story celebrates a defining moment in the agency's development. Sharing this story empowers the organization to express its identity internally to its employees and externally to its clients, advocates, and supporters in an authentic way. To an employee at the Kinship Center, picture how this story contributes to creating an environment pulsing with determination and conviction. The story fuels the imaginations of employees. Equipped with the story, employees gain a tangible anchor for the ongoing challenges of performing their jobs in a meaningful way. The story provides emotional fuel.

Theme #2: Courage

Sam and Maria Gonzalez wanted to adopt a healthy infant. They were not prepared for heartbreak and losses on the way to becoming parents. Sam and Maria, second-generation members of an immigrant family, are a straightforward, hardworking couple living in a rural California community. They had family and community support from their small hometown for their adoption. The Kinship Center staff was enthusiastic about helping this engaging couple achieve their goal to be parents.

Birth parents selected them for adoption of their unborn child. Sam and Maria spent time with and learned to respect the birth parents. When the child was born, the birth parents confirmed their adoption decision and the baby went home with Sam and Maria. Within two months, the birth parents were unable to keep to their decision and reclaimed the infant. The pain was immeasurable, but the Gonzalezes honored the birth parents' change of mind.

It was not long before the birth parents called again and said that they could not manage the responsibility of parenting and wanted Sam and Maria to take the child back. After considerable counseling to assess the birth parents' situation and to measure the risk, Sam and Maria accepted the infant again. Within weeks, the birth parents reclaimed the child permanently, and the Gonzalezes were brokenhearted yet again. The birth parents expressed their sincere regret for the pain that was caused to the adopting family, but they were firm in their decision.

Such sad stories happen in adoption, but they always bring emotional and ethical conflict to the adopting families and to the agency staff. In adoption, it is accepted that young birth parents are in crisis and would otherwise be raising their child; that all of the adults involved take the burden of uncertainty for the sake of the child and accept responsibility for making decisions that have uncertain outcomes. There is, however, no way to fully prepare an adopting family for the pain of losing a child they have come to love and believe to be part of their family.

Sam and Maria became parents within a year, being chosen again to adopt a child who had already been born. Their courage and determination helped them to achieve a complete family unit with two wonderful children. To our knowledge, the first child in this story is doing well with his birth family. He may never need to know the story of his early beginnings.

This is only one example of the stress to both families and social work staff that are part of the adoption story. It is not possible to weigh and measure the courage, the challenges, the pain, and the unpredictability that are a part of daily life for those working in child welfare. The mission of ensuring that a child who needs a family will have one must be stronger than the need for control and certainty in the work that is done on behalf of children. There is knowledge and art to the field, but there is no roadmap to certain outcomes.

Discussion

Imagine sitting down with a couple preparing to adopt a child. How would you prepare them for the emotional journey? This story of courage becomes a critical backdrop for empowering a social worker to paint a vivid picture. For couples considering adoption, the story provides a tool for their thinking. Through the story, social workers can help couples vicariously consider multiple perspectives. It is a tool for thinking about the child, the birth parents, themselves, and the demands placed on a social worker who is attempting to facilitate a successful outcome for all parties involved.

Theme #3: Belief and Staying Power

Amos was referred to a specialized foster care program that worked with children who presented extreme behavioral and emotional challenges. This young adolescent with no permanent family connections had been unsuccessfully placed in several foster and institutional settings prior to coming to the Kinship Center. He was far behind in school, had challenging learning disabilities, and his progress in social and academic learning was affected by his serious emotional problems. His chances for an independent and productive adulthood were not promising.

Despite the bleak prospects for his future, Amos graduated from high school, but not without difficulties and setbacks. He was not discharged from foster care and left to survive on his own. Instead, he was guided to enroll in the Job Corps and has successfully completed training as a licensed vocational nurse. At age 21, he is now living independently and maintaining a good work record.

What were the ingredients that changed the chemistry of Amos's future? Two caring and concerned adults who have maintained a lasting commitment to him made the difference between losing this youth into the impermanence of the foster care system and helping him to develop belief in himself.

Clarice, his Kinship Center social worker, has been Amos's constant mentor and coach for over six years. His single-parent foster mother, Mary, has made a lifetime commitment to being his family and did not wither during the difficult years. How did these two women maintain a strong support system? They became a dedicated team on behalf of one youth. They did so with the support of a strong organization that underscored their belief, that provided more than the basic resources for their work, and continued a commitment to Amos after he left the foster care system. Amos continues to receive letters and calls, visits his foster mother, and receives minimal but sustaining financial support from his former foster family agency. Someone always remembers his birthday and holidays. His future is not yet secure, but he has entered young adulthood in a positive way that would not have been predicted given his tumultuous childhood and his emotional challenges.

Discussion

This story illustrates the staying power of a concerned agency and the belief in a positive outcome by an involved adult. Hearing the story, the listener (or reader) will not easily forget Amos and the Kinship Center.

Theme #4: Keeping the Course and Being Firm

Jessie's early life was with a mother who was addicted to drugs. There was no stable family unit, no consistent place to live, and many dangerous adults in and out of her mother's life. Some of them abused Jessie. She came into foster care at age seven after showing up at a local school because Big Bird said that girls and boys should go to school. An investigation uncovered her desperate living conditions and brought her into court custody.

This child was blessed with an outgoing personality that endeared her to everyone who met her. She also had learned behaviors that included stealing, lying, and manipulating. She held onto her streetwise behaviors for a very long time. Jessie was a survivor, and despite having a loving foster family, she constantly tested their commitment to her.

The key to helping Jessie blossom was constant structure and consistency from every adult in her life. She had years of therapy, firm but loving discipline, and she learned best from the logical outcomes for her misbehaviors. Slowly, she began to thrive. Her early academic achievements were promising. Jessie was always reaching for new goals and was supported to gain them.

Her social worker, Gayle, was a constant force in Jessie's life for 10 years. Seeing her promise, Gayle reached for amazing resources for Jessie. She single-handedly sought and achieved a full scholarship for Jessie to attend a prestigious private high school. Her early performance at the private school was spotty, but key faculty members supported her, and the Kinship Center provided tutoring and other financial aid. By eleventh grade, she had overcome the early learning deficits and ultimately graduated with a 3.2 grade point average (GPA). Jessie believed that she had taken charge of her life and could achieve her dreams.

She was assisted with applying to college and was eligible for significant financial aid if she stayed in California, including some from the Kinship Center's scholarship program. Jessie insisted that she wanted to attend one, and only one, college of her choice—a distant university where there was not a local support system. It was at this point that all of the prior structure that had been provided to Jessie broke down. Despite all of the adults' beliefs that she should stay in California and attend a nearby college or university, Jessie persisted in her dream and was supported to strike out on her own and attend the distant school. Disaster followed.

Jessie dropped out of college in her sophomore year. Her determination faltered. She had no local support system, financial hardships followed because her academic performance in the private college did not entitle her to additional scholarship aid, and she had difficulty making friends. She felt as if she had failed herself. Instead of responding to pleas to come back to California and start over at a local school, Jessie retreated and severed contact with all of the adults who cared about her.

Ultimately, she resurfaced in the same city and neighborhood where she had begun. She is now a single parent to several children and struggling economically. Her former social worker and family have lost contact with her. Jessie is a strong person, and the participation of many in guiding her childhood toward positive outcomes will contribute to her ability to manage her life.

Discussion

Carol Biddle had this to say about the story: "The lesson that Jessie has given our agency is an understanding of the importance of maintaining a good plan and staying the course until the job is done. I share this story with employees to emphasize the critical nature of maintaining the delicate balance between flexibility and structure. Ultimately, the caring adults and the organization that supported Jessie succumbed to her charm and supported a course of action that was not practical, not predictable of success, and led to a breakdown of the structures that had kept her safe and promoted her steady achievement. But there are no regrets. Jessie deserved every opportunity and all of the effort put into her development. Ultimately, she is again experiencing the logical outcomes of poor choices."

Theme #5: Love and Resilience

Nancy Webster had always wanted a daughter. She and Bob had two healthy sons, ages 11 and 12. Nancy told her husband that she wanted to adopt a child. He thought it was an unusual request. Everyone was happy with the way things were.

Nancy began to do research and quickly contacted a local agency that specialized in international adoption. The agency completed a home study and connected the Websters to an organization that matched children in eastern European orphanages with American families. In July 2000, a small group of five-year-old children accompanied by a representative of an orphanage in an Eastern region of what was once the Soviet Union, arrived in Southern California for a five-week visit. The weary children had been on four airplane flights over the course of two days.

As the children came into the airport waiting area, some cried or threw tantrums in exhaustion. Some looked blankly at the sea of strange faces in front of them. Sasha stood out. The most vivacious of the group, lively and excited, she had no time for tears. Her big blue eyes scanned the faces, and Nancy felt a rush of warmth in her heart for this brave little girl.

Sasha came home to stay with Nancy, Bob, Joe, and Tim for five weeks. They lived in a whirlwind of activities. They went to Disneyland and Magic Mountain, ate ice cream and pizza, attended parties, and looked at the ocean. The Websters showed Sasha many new wonderful things and places and tried to do all the things that a family could possibly do with a little girl who had spent her entire life inside the walls of an orphanage. Nancy also took Sasha to see a pediatrician who has a special interest in children adopted internationally. When Dr. Minke asked Nancy how Sasha acted, Nancy said honestly, "she's wild." Although small, Sasha appeared to be in fine physical health. They talked about plans to bring Sasha back for further assessment when the adoption was final.

The five weeks came to a quick end. It didn't seem possible that the all the little children were now going back to the orphanage so far away. Nancy knew that Sasha was part of the family now and she would do whatever was necessary to bring her back to stay. Nancy called Sasha at the orphanage every two weeks with a translator on the phone as well. Administrative problems, paperwork, and more paperwork delayed Nancy and Bob's trip to the orphanage where Sasha lived and waited. After a year and a half of waiting, word finally came that Nancy and Bob had permission to go and get their little girl.

Nancy and Bob spent eight days together with Sasha in a one-room apartment in the local city near the orphanage. Bob had to return to his job in the United States. Nancy spent another 35 days with Sasha, just the two of them, mother and daughter. Sasha, thin and pale, was in constant motion and always happy and delighted with everything she saw. Nancy saw the large bald spot on top of Sasha's head where one of the older girls from the orphanage had systematically pulled out Sasha's hair. Her energy seemed overwhelming to Nancy, who was calm and easygoing. The only information Nancy had about Sasha was the paperwork from the orphanage. Sasha had been abandoned at the orphanage door when she was one month old. The names of her family were not known. The doctor she consulted through the orphanage verified the only facts that Nancy knew about Sasha. Sasha had received her shots, and, yes, it was true that she had a happy disposition.

Nancy and Sasha boarded the train at the outskirts of Sasha's hometown. The forbidding mountains and the vast open spaces vanished behind them as the train chugged for hours across the steppes. Then, they were in Moscow, and Sasha stayed in a hotel room for the first time. The sights and sounds of the city overwhelmed her. Then she was on a plane with her mother bound for the United States, leaving behind forever the other children she had played with, the only family she had ever known.

Within a few days, rested from the trip, Nancy and Bob settled in to parent their new daughter. She seemed to fit right in with the family routines. And she was never afraid. Nancy marveled at her. Sasha started summer school two weeks after her arrival, picking up English right away. She lost her accent almost immediately. Nancy continually offered to help Sasha, but she brushed off the help and did the work on her own. Testing by the school soon after she arrived concluded that she was doing so well that she didn't need help with reading, tutoring, speech, or language. Learning was not a problem.

Sasha gained weight slowly and began to display a talent for athletics. In fact, Nancy saw her daughter developing an ability that went beyond the talents of her new brothers. Her balance was great, her muscles were well developed, and she wasn't afraid of anything, it seemed. Nancy began to see that her daughter was really a tough cookie. Sasha didn't get upset and took things as they came. She was rarely sad and wanted to help everyone, always trying to be kind.

Slowly, other traits began to show up in Sasha's behavior. She was hyperactive, going from activity to activity without stopping. She had trouble being alone and was very outgoing, never afraid of anyone. She would talk to anyone. She had a sense of humor and loved to play. And she was very, very stubborn.

Nancy worked very hard to get to know Sasha. Gradually, Nancy began to learn about the caretakers in Sasha's orphanage. They watched X-rated movies in front of the kids every night. Sasha, it seemed, had a curiosity about anything related to sex. She explained the pornography she had seen in graphic detail. She talked about her past and said she didn't want to ever go back. She told Nancy and Bob and her brothers how happy she was to have a family and to be in America.

A year passed. One day, Nancy got a call from a friend whose young daughter often played with Sasha. The friend was distraught after her daughter had disclosed that Sasha had engaged her in sexual play. Nancy couldn't believe it was true. Then Nancy learned that Sasha had been sneaking and watching an adult cable channel with sexually explicit programming as well.

Nancy began putting together all the information she had about Sasha's behavior. Her research and discussion with other parents of adoptees from the orphanage led her to seek professional help. She contacted Dr. Minke, who referred her to the Kinship Center. The Kinship Center counselor listened carefully to Nancy's concerns and helped her talk about her experiences parenting Sasha. Meeting Sasha for the first time, the counselor saw a tanned, healthy little girl with wise, sad eyes. Sasha was terrified of talking to the counselor. She stood stiffly next to her mother, painfully shy and worried about this new experience.

Gradually, with her mother at her side, sometimes holding her hand or rubbing her back, Sasha began to talk a little more, to draw pictures about her life and eventually sit on the sofa with her mom. Sasha began to tell stories about her life in the orphanage. She described eating the same white porridge every day. She said she learned not to complain about anything because if she did, she would have to take off her shoes. Then she would get hit with her own shoes by one of the orphanage caretakers. She shared memories of leaving the orphanage, feeling so amazed and surprised that her dream had come true, that she had a real family to live with.

One day in counseling Sasha talked about her upcoming birthday. She was full of excitement. The counselor learned that Sasha had never had a birthday before she came to live with her adoptive parents. The excitement was so great that Nancy reported Sasha spent her entire birthday playing and refused to eat all day.

Discussion

Carol Biddle had this to say about the story: "This brave little girl's story reminds us all of the strength and resiliency of the human spirit. Her life experiences were limited to the four walls of an institution for the first six years of her life. She struggles with self-esteem, with her identity, and with the daily experiences of being a youngster in a modern, changing society. She continues to learn to trust and to learn to give and receive affection. Many of the life lessons that a much younger child would learn from a parent have to be repeated for Sasha at an older age because she never had a chance to learn those lessons for the first time. And Sasha practices gratitude every day, saying " I love you," every chance she has, to her mom, dad, and big brothers for giving her the family she always dreamed she might have one day. The elements of the story that impress us with the ideas of love and resilience include the imagery of the long train ride across the steppes. What is more resilient than mountains? The slow, patient growth of this family's relationship with Sasha perfectly reflects how love can overcome severe problems. Telling this story helps our agency to reflect the themes of love and resilience and conveys one of the agency's most powerful messages."

A FINAL STORY ABOUT HOW THE KINSHIP CENTER WORKS WITH STORIES FROM CAROL BIDDLE

When Carol Biddle was sharing with me thoughts on how she uses story, she immediately thought of the agency's caregiver program. This last story provides some background on the Family Ties program and explores how stories have been a central communication for Carol and the agency to discuss the work of this agency program.

The unsung heroes who are making permanent families for children who would otherwise be in foster care are the grandmothers of America. It was amazing for the Kinship Center staff to discover that there were more than 500 children enrolled in a relative caregiver program in the small California county of Monterey. We were asked by the local social services department to rescue the languishing program that was not meeting the stated goals or needs. The Kinship Center agreed to do so, because we believe firmly that permanency in a related family is the best option for children who cannot remain with their birth parents. The program added a new wrinkle to our mission and has become an integral part of our work.

We would like to report that the services to grandparents and other relatives were a part of our strategic plan. However, we discovered this part of our mission by default rather than by design. Having spent 17 years working to achieve and support permanency for children in a family, relatives were not on our radarscope. Slowly, the grandparents began migrating to our education programs, support groups, and mental health clinics in increasing numbers. By 2002, we discovered that about 35 percent of our clients statewide were relatives, mostly fixed- and low-income grandparents who had no other source of services and support.

Many gifts come wrapped in packages that one does not immediately appreciate. Such was the case with Family Ties, the relative caregiver program. Once the Kinship Center assumed responsibility for the program, it learned that the funding was going to expire in less than two years. This was definitely a "gotcha," because by the time it figured this out, the Kinship Center was firmly hooked.

Family Ties had services and staffing that were unlike existing programs. Many staff members were themselves relative caregivers, bringing a new paraprofessional group to enrich the organization in ways they could not have imagined. We learn lessons every day from their practical approach to enabling and assisting families. They are definitely not clinically oriented, as are most of our other programs. The Family Ties program returned us to basic social work and our own version of a neighborhood community center experience. As a result, administrators and board members have energetically refocused on achieving funding and donations for clothing, food, holiday support, tutoring, recreation, respite care for elderly caregivers, as well as the familiar services such as caregiver education and child mental health services.

Board members and the executive director of the Kinship Center are frequent storytellers to the general community in an effort to gain support for the work they do. The relative caregiver stories never fail to resonate with listeners. Almost everyone immediately relates to how hard it is for an older relative to have an unplanned second or third generation of children descend upon them at the worst possible moment, without preparation, and without resources that they may have been able to garner at an earlier age. Almost everyone knows or knows of someone to whom this unexpected life experience has happened. Most often, the story is connected to an adult child who has become his or her own victim of substance abuse and neglect of their children. Everyone, universally, does not want this to happen to themselves or to the grandparents they know. The story transcends income levels, educational levels, and cultures. It brings most people to tears and the remainder to thoughtful concern. It is the best story to illustrate the importance of family and the need for community awareness and support. People who do not understand foster care or adoption understand grandparents who make another place at the table, even when the table is bare.

This is a universal storyline found in relative caregiver situations: Imagine that you are a 50- or 60-something grandmother, single, with health problems, a fixed- or poverty-level income, in a small one-bedroom apartment. You get a call from the sheriff's department in the middle of the night, telling you that your three grandchildren are in their custody and about to be placed in separate emergency foster homes with strangers. You are informed that your son or daughter is arrested and will be sentenced to drug and alcohol rehabilitation or might even go to prison. The sheriff (or social worker) tells you that you have been identified as the only known and safe relative to receive the children. What do you do? Of course, you go and get your grandchildren, bring them home, love them, and decide to worry tomorrow about what will happen next.

Discussion

The administrators of the Kinship Center use empathy as a powerful technique when seeking support for the relative caregivers program. In telling the story, they help listeners feel the struggles of an older person trying to keep a family together, despite hardship.

SUMMARY

Effective communication results in understanding and learning. The Kinship Center's stories are essential vehicles for the agency. Through the stories, much can be learned about what makes the agency tick. These stories empower its members to speak about their work and create a vibrant culture. It's not enough to say the stories are motivating, because they function in ways that go far beyond that. The stories illustrate how stories empower communication with external and internal audiences by encoding information and acting as tools for thinking.

3 / *Managing through Stories*

SO MUCH HAS been written about the "art" and "science" of management. In our heart of hearts, we know there are no 10 steps to becoming a better manager. We are guilty of gobbling up whatever latest quick-fix fad is out there while we console ourselves for falling short of finding the holy grail of management. People are not simple. When you put lots of them together with the aim of rallying around an organization's mission, everyone's needs, desires, and fears muddy the waters. Complicated theories will not lift the shroud of mystery, but simple principles out of which very complex behaviors emerge are our best hope. Stories are not the unified theory of management, but they do offer us some important clues about communication and relationships.

The challenges of managing people and processes are mitigated by the power of stories. In the last two chapters we learned how stories play a crucial role in communication by empowering a speaker, encoding information, and acting as a tool for thinking. Communication is the foundation for managing, and stories are one of the best ways to understand the mechanisms of effective communication. This chapter examines two more functions of stories: stories require active listening, and stories help us negotiate differences. Our pursuit of better management practices can be achieved if we learn to listen actively to the stories around us, and if we use these stories to negotiate our differences.

STORIES REQUIRE ACTIVE LISTENING

Let's begin our discussion of managing through stories by examining how stories require active listening. Do you ever feel like you are not heard or understood?

It's no surprise that our relationships at work and at home are often riddled with problems. We do a horrible job of listening to each other. To make matters worse, we do not treat our experiences with circumspection; therefore, we fail to gain insights and learn from them. We stumble along oblivious to other people's perspectives and unaware of what experiences have contributed to the development of the perceptual filters that color each person's worldview. If we had to deal with only our own worldview, we might not care, but this inaccessible, foggy filter also guides the behavior of others.

The following short story provides a glimpse of the problems that occur when we become engrossed in our own perceptions:

The Train Story

Four travelers shared a train compartment: a beautiful young woman, the young woman's grandmother, a distinguished general, and a young officer. As the train sped along at night, the lights in the compartment suddenly went off. In the darkness, two distinct sounds could be heard from the compartment: the sound of a wet juicy kiss and the sound of a hand slapping the side of a face. When the lights came back on, the faces of the travelers told a story. The young woman's face was red from embarrassment. She was mortified to think that the young man had kissed her in the dark. She was very thankful that she was traveling with her grandmother, who slapped the young man. The grandmother's hands were clenched in fists of rage and she was fuming. She could not believe that the general would try to take advantage of her granddaughter, but she was glad she had taught her granddaughter to never let a man touch her without permission. Her granddaughter had done the right thing to slap that dirty old man. The veins in the general's neck were bulging. He was furious. He had tried to teach the young officer about respect and discipline. The general couldn't believe that the young whippersnapper had kissed the beautiful woman, who then mistakenly had slapped the general. The young man was grinning from ear to ear. He couldn't believe his good fortune. How often do you get to kiss a beautiful young woman and slap your boss at the same time?

Everyone is mixed up in this story except for our friend the young officer. Emotions run high and the characters are operating literally and figuratively in the dark. Isn't this story representative of how we are guilty of acting sometimes? We seldom know the "real story" behind someone's feelings, beliefs, or actions. Worse yet, we do not make the effort to discover their story. Convinced of our opinions, we prefer to keep our mental world neat and orderly by staying focused on our perspective rather than entertaining another point of view. Although these natural proclivities of our mind are assets intended by evolution to equip our species with the ability to act independently and decisively, they are also liabilities when it comes to relationships. When we actively listen to other people's stories we do not need to abandon our ideas; instead we can enter a new frame of reference by reconstituting the story being shared with us in our minds and hearts. Stories allow us to move in and out of a different frame of reference. We are, in essence, "standing in someone else's shoes."

Management has come to mean "control" to many people. If we cannot control something or someone, how can we manage it? Relationships cannot be controlled. We have to learn how to get in pace with each other, and we have to work at it. Yet managing is all about relationships, and relationships depend on open lines of communication. We cannot enact a policy to ensure that people take the time and effort to hear one another. We must model these behaviors and invest a tremendous amount of energy and patience into sustaining these fragile conduits. Stories turn out to be a great tool for accomplishing this.

Hearing someone else's story may not change our perspective, but it opens up dialogue and increases the chance of a mutually satisfying resolution. Although we may not become expert listeners overnight, stories help us understand each other's perspective because they require active listening. Stories catapult our imaginations into new directions. Many of our habitual ways of looking at things can be altered by a story's capacity to engage us. Our connection to others and our understanding of their perspectives is deepened by a story's ability to inform us in ways that words by themselves cannot do.

I was introduced to the concept of "active listening" by my father, Theodore, who is a conductor and composer. I love sitting by his side while he pores over an orchestra score. Of course, to me the notes on the page are little more than an abstraction. But to my father, they are a rich sea of sound and emotion. With his eyes, Theodore "hears" all of the instruments playing the music perfectly. He is quick to remind me that Beethoven wrote his Ninth Symphony when he was deaf. Theodore insists that not even the greatest recording of the Ninth Symphony can come close to what Beethoven must have heard in his head.

I remember watching my father conduct orchestra rehearsals. He begins his first rehearsal with any orchestra by saying, "If I cannot speak to you with this baton, we're both in trouble!" And while my father said very little, he communicated a lot, and he listened intently. Even during the loudest section of music, when all of the instruments are playing *forte,* my father can isolate the sound of one violinist playing the wrong sharp or flat. Communicating with one another would be a lot easier if we all had such exceptional listening skills.

Take a moment to consider why the same piece of music evokes different emotions in different people. Could it be that the emotive power of music is tied to people's memories, stories, and the associations they make? In this respect, stories and music are very similar. Stories have multiple threads. Stories do not grow old.

However, our imagination grows lazy. We need to challenge ourselves. Is it possible for us to find a new nugget of gold each time we hear or relay a story? Can we find an unturned rock, a new nuance? To do so, we must develop the capacity for active listening.

I am reminded of the wonderful cliché:

> A wise old owl lived in an oak; the more he saw, the less he spoke; the less he spoke, the more he heard. Why can't we all be like that wise old bird?

What we need is less doing and more listening. But the amount of each is a hard thing to quantify. The results are undeniable but they somehow evade direct observation. Like a tree that changes color in the fall and loses its leaves in winter, the transformations are imperceptible on a daily basis, but when viewed from a seasonal perspective the results are staggering.

Managing is an art of bringing our attention into the moment. Like the wise old owl, the more we strive to hear people's stories, the more we will be able to manage by not managing. Put another way, as we listen to each other's stories, it becomes possible to negotiate differences. More often than not, our conflicts are a function of not hearing and understanding one another. Spontaneous solutions and resolutions arise when we enter someone else's frame of reference. Sharing our stories generates vivid pictures for others, because when we listen actively we bring our experiences to their telling. Therefore, a bridge of understanding is constructed between two or more people. The greatest challenge for managers is to create an environment of genuine interest, trust, openness, and reciprocity where people willingly share their stories.

If there is only one concept from this book you put into action let it be this:

> By eliciting other people's stories and your own and actively listening to them, you will improve communications and build satisfying, productive, rewarding relationships in all areas of your life.

Vignette #4: The Red Handkerchief

Joe walked briskly to the auditorium. He loved teaching the MBA seminar on leadership. Today's topic was going to be tricky. How could he convey to the class the elusive concepts of active listening and empathy and their importance to leadership? As he made his way to the front of the room, he decided to tell the class one of his favorite stories. When the students had settled into their seats, he began.

"Once upon time there was a mighty king by the name of Stephan. Now Stephan had almost everything: land, wealth, and tremendous power. Sadly, Stephan was missing one thing: a wife. One day he turned to his chief advisor and said, 'You have the most beautiful daughter in the land. My life is complete, but I need a companion. I will marry your daughter. Go tell her my wishes. We must arrange a stupendous wedding feast as soon as possible.'

"The chief advisor went home in terror. He knew his daughter was very picky about the men she dated. What if she would not marry the king? The king would have his head for sure. Cautiously, the chief advisor approached his daughter Zalea and began his plea.

"'My dear Zalea, I have great news to share with you. The king wants to marry you. Isn't that wonderful?' Without pausing to take a breath or look into his daughter's eyes, he continued, 'I'll run back to the palace to tell the king you have accepted his proposal.'

"'Father, wait,' began Zalea. 'How could I possibly marry the king? I neither know nor love him. I am flattered by his proposal, but I cannot possibly accept it.'

"The chief advisor's face contorted with pain. 'Zalea, your poor father's head may be at stake here. You don't want to disappoint the king, do you? He is such a wonderful king and employer. Think of all the perks you will have as queen. I don't think it is a career opportunity you should pass up.'

"Zalea's face lit up. 'You're right, father. I know the king has a reputation as a good man, but he is young and lacks any marketable skills. Tell the king I will accept his proposal on one, and only one, condition.'

"The chief advisor's face relaxed. 'And what might that be?'

"Looking her father square in the eye, and with the autocratic tone of a queen, she said, 'The king must learn a trade. When he can demonstrate to me that he has a marketable skill, then I will accept his proposal.'

"The chief advisor's face became sullen. He recognized the tone of voice. His daughter had made up her mind and there would be no changing it. Slowly he walked back to the palace.

"Once there, the chief advisor did everything he could to avoid the king. Finally, the king tracked him down. 'Where have you been? I have been looking all over the palace for you. Tell me your daughter's decision.'

"'Well, Your Highness,' the chief advisor said, 'my daughter will gladly accept your proposal. However, she had one little request. Zalea wants you to learn a trade.'

"'A what?' roared the king.

"'A trade, Your Highness.' Fearing the worst, the chief advisor closed his eyes and pressed his hands together in prayer.

"'Hmm,' muttered the king. 'Chief advisor, I know now that your daughter is as wise as she is beautiful. I will fulfill her wish. Tomorrow I will begin to search for a trade to learn.'

"The chief advisor let out a huge sigh of relief and ran all the way home to tell his daughter the news.

"Over the next few days, the king observed and spoke to all sorts of craftsmen. He watched the marketing and advertising department haggle over product positioning and branding. He listened to overbearing sales pitches. He yawned uncontrollably as the bean counters in the accounting department verified his financial position, and he came close to losing his lunch as he listened to technologists in the information technology department frenetically espouse their e-commerce strategies. Finally, the king found an old weaver who began to show him the intricacies of his trade.

"The king worked at his loom night and day to learn his new trade. One day he called in his chief advisor to show him a splendid scarf he had woven. The scarf showed a red rose on a dark, forest-green background. The king asked his chief advisor to take the scarf to Zalea as a gift. When Zalea saw it she knew the king had learned the trade of weaving. Happily, she agreed to marry him, and there was a grand and joyous celebration.

"The king quickly learned that his wife was indeed very wise. He sought her advice on all the kingdom's affairs. One day he said to Zalea, 'I don't know what people in our kingdom want, or how they feel. I cannot rely on my advisors. They tell me what they think I want to hear. How can I learn to be sensitive to my people's needs?'

"'My dear,' Zalea began, 'you must walk in your people's shoes. Go to the market dressed as a common person. As you wander, listen to what people say to one another. Then I believe you will find answers to your questions.'

"So the king and some of his advisors disguised themselves and made their way to the market. As they strolled along, the king was amazed at what he learned. Around noon, the king turned to his advisors and said, 'I'm hungry. Lets get a bite to eat.'

"'Marvelous!' responded his chief advisor. Let's get out of these dingy clothes and head back to the palace for a proper meal.'

"'No,' the king retorted. 'I want to eat like the people in my kingdom. I overheard people talking about an excellent greasy spoon known for its burgers and Philly cheesesteak sandwiches. Let's go eat there.'

"The king led the way while his advisors sheepishly followed him. They arrived at the restaurant. As they tried to enter, a trap door opened beneath them and they fell into a deep, dark pit. Moments later the trap door opened and a hideous man snarled at them as he threw burgers down for them to eat. 'Now you know why I have the best burgers in the kingdom. My burgers are made from fat, plump people like you.' The man slammed the trap door shut and went away laughing.

"'What do we do now?' moaned one advisor.

"'We are as good as dead,' whimpered another.

"'Listen, Your Highness,' the chief advisor said, 'you'd better tell that idiot who we are. That will end this nonsense.'

"'Quiet, all of you!' yelled the king. 'If we tell this evil man who we are, we are as good as dead. Now, leave me alone for a moment. I need to think. None of you must utter a word the next time he comes.'

"A good deal later the trap door opened. 'Eat up, lads. I have lots of hungry customers to feed,' bellowed the evil man.

"'Excuse me, sir,' the king chimed in. 'I know you can't set us free, but my life is so precious to me. I can weave the most beautiful scarves you have ever seen. The queen at the palace pays great sums of money for them. Surely you realize that we can earn you more money by weaving scarves than you will earn from the measly burgers you can make from our bodies. If you give me a loom and some red and green yarn, I will show you how I can make you a richer man.'

"'I'll think about it,' snorted the evil man. A few minutes later, the trap door opened and the evil man threw down a loom and some yarn for the king.

"The king worked all night. He wove a beautiful scarf with a red rose on a dark, forest-green background. In the morning he gave it to the evil man, saying, 'Take this scarf to Queen Zalea. She will pay you a handsome price for it.'

"The evil man ran all the way to the palace. The palace had been in total chaos since the king and his advisors had disappeared. When Zalea saw the scarf, she immediately recognized the work of her husband. She paid the evil man four pieces of gold and gave him stock options worth a good deal more. When the evil man left, Zalea had the king's army follow him.

"She herself rode at the head of the army. When they reached the evil man's restaurant, the army seized all of his assets, instructed the Justice Department to break up his franchise, told the executioner to cut off his head, and freed the king and his advisors. And Zalea and the king rode off together into the sunset and lived happily ever after."

Questions for Reflection

Before reading any further, take a few moments to think about the following questions:

1. What are some examples of active listening from the story?
2. Why does Zalea want the king to learn a trade?
3. How is the image of weaving related to active listening?

Analysis

King Stephan learns the value of active listening. When Zalea instructs the king to learn a trade before she will marry him, he recognizes Zalea's wisdom. He realizes that, although he is a powerful king, he has no specific skills. So he goes on a fact-finding mission.

One of the joys of stories is that they can evolve and adapt themselves to fit the audience to whom they are told. This story is being told to business school students, so our storyteller weaves in references and associations that will pique their interest.

The king discovers that there are many aspects of his kingdom and its people about which he knows nothing. He sets out on a discovery mission and decides to learn the art of weaving. Mastering any new skill requires time, patience, and a lot of active listening. The king is taking a vital first step toward better understanding his people. In many cultures, weavers are depicted as storytellers. By learning the art of weaving, the king is getting in touch with himself, his stories, and, ultimately, his people.

Once the king and Zalea are married, he relies heavily on her for advice. He asks her a simple but profound question: What do his people think and feel? Zalea's response captures the essence of active listening. She tells the king, "You must walk in your people's shoes." Zalea is helping her husband develop compassion and empathy. When the king walks as a commoner among his people, he is amazed by what he hears and learns. The king succeeds in adopting a new frame of reference. He has effectively suspended his royal perspective and embraced the perspective of the people in his kingdom.

When we succeed in listening actively to each other's stories, and consider our own response to them, we enter into a new realm of understanding. We become capable of embracing contradictions and paradoxes. We become aware of competing thoughts, feelings, and emotions. And unlike the "rational mind," the "story mind" can entertain all of these possibilities without experiencing any dissonance.

Returning to the story, we see the king use his newfound wisdom and his trade when he and his advisors get caught by the evil man. The king does not use force. He knows that neither force nor his social position will get him out of his predicament. Quite the contrary. The king must be cunning. In the end, it is the king's ability to listen actively that saves him and reunites him with his wise and beautiful wife.

Active listening plays a critical role in verbal and written communications. The next story is about a memo. Behind the sound business recommendations of this memo is subtext.

Vignette #5: Capital Success Training Company

Capital Success Training Company is undergoing changes to solidify its competitive place in the market. Before reading the vignette, here are some key facts:

- *Trainers are contract employees. They receive a per-day fee for leading seminars as well as a commission on goods sold during the event.*
- *Over 95 percent of the seminars are one day in length.*
- *Capital Success uses a per-capita commission schedule for products sold.*
- *Prior to the new policy changes introduced in the memo below, trainers were always provided with an assistant at every seminar and a shipment of books, tapes, and resource materials for participants to browse and for trainers to sell.*

Clyde read his memo one last time. As long as he was in control, he would do whatever it took to put Capital Success Training on the map. Since 1990, the company had contracted over 350 trainers to teach 45 classes. During the last three years, Clyde had increased the company's revenues by 60 percent by introducing the sale of books, videos, and audiotapes during classes.

Leo sighed as he opened the memo from Capital Success Training. It was difficult to stay on top of all of the company's changes. Since Leo had started, he had learned how to be an effective salesman. At every class he taught, he set up a sales table in the back of the room to display the products Capital Success Training shipped to him. Leo was not fond of sales, but with the help of an assistant he usually managed to sell enough to make a decent commission. In a few minutes he was supposed to meet a group of Capital Success trainers for a drink. He reread the memo in the meantime. It read as follows:

FROM: Clyde Clawson
TO: Capital Success Trainers
SUBJECT: New Sales Policies

Everyone has been working very hard. As we continue to grow, I want to go over some new policies. Here is a summary of what we need to do:

1. Tighten up the product list of books, tapes, and audiotapes sold at our classes.
2. Review which classes to ship products to.
3. Eliminate sales-administrative assistants for classes with low attendance.
4. Evaluate trainers based on their class evaluations and sales results.

To some of you, these changes may sound drastic, unfair, arbitrary, demeaning, punitive, or pick the complaining adjective of your choice. You're entitled to your own opinion, of course, but make sure you understand and consider the facts before you jump to conclusions.

We are financially solid, and our market share continues to grow. Those of you who watch our competition know they've been declining in number of classes presented, number of employees, and number of trainers contracted. We continue to grow in all categories.

We believe we'll stay ahead of the pack by making proactive, smart business decisions before economic or market conditions force us to make reactive, defensive ones. As long as we can protect and nurture the best features of our business by culling the worst, we're going to remain healthy.

How all of this might impact you personally is up to you. If you're thinking, "Hey, my sales are always good, so I won't see much change," you're right. Or if you're thinking, "Well, I can learn how to sell out of the catalog as long as I've got samples to show," you're right, too, and you'll probably get your sales back up to the point where shipping isn't a question! But if your reaction is, "They won't buy anything if they can't take it with them," I'd guess you're one of the trainers who hasn't sold much of anything under any conditions. If that continues to be a convenient excuse, I'll miss working with you.

Once the urge to call and play the "ain't it awful" game with your best trainer friend or most insightful assistant has passed, please call me. I've got lots of great ideas on how we all can prosper from product sales!

As our business evolves and grows to meet the demands of the marketplace, change is inevitable. We make little adjustments all the time, as you know, because that's the kind of quick-response management that allows us to stay strong and keep growing. To make sure we're always moving forward, always giving our customers what they want, and always providing trainers with opportunities to train and always operating as cost-effectively as possible, some conditions demand more extensive change:

1. Trainers with the best sales results will be scheduled to teach workshops first.
2. We'll ship products to your classes when your sales history on that topic and the projected attendance for that class indicate that your effort will generate enough sales to at least cover costs. Some classes will not have products shipped to them.
3. Every class and every trainer will receive product catalogs, along with all the support we can muster to help everyone sell well. As your sales improve, so will your chances of having products shipped.
4. We're designing training programs to help you learn new techniques for selling from display samples and catalogs. You remain eligible to earn the established commission rates for each class, regardless of whether products are in the room.
5. For all classes in which you will be acting as your own program manager, we will pay you an additional commission of 2 percent on the day's sales. And, yes, in response to several of you who've asked, you may, with our advance approval, choose to be your own assistant in a high-attendance class when we can be assured customer service won't be sacrificed.

To be very frank, the better your sales record, the fewer changes you'll experience. Even for training topics for which we normally wouldn't ship product, you'll still have every opportunity to prove that your sales performance warrants our going to the expense of doing so. We both benefit when you're successful at product sales.

Trainers who've been achieving excellent sales results will see very little, if any, change as a result of these new procedures. Trainers who've been struggling with sales but working with us to improve will be supported as long as they're making progress with sales that pay their way. Trainers who don't produce acceptable sales results, who don't demonstrate any effort, or who just don't care will find that we will match their level. They certainly won't get any products at their classes, and if their inability to produce sales persists, they may find that our ability to schedule them for classes has ended.

We are working on a variety of programs to help you boost your sales. A final note: Please don't become the victim of rumor or gossip. As trees grow, they need to be pruned so that dead wood doesn't slow the advance of strong branches and leaves. That's exactly what, and only what, we're doing. Tree branches, however, don't have the luxury of choosing their own destiny. You do. When you need more explanation or have questions, ask me. Let's work hard together to keep our growth going.

Leo folded the memo in half and stuck it in his pocket. He wondered what the other trainers would say about Clyde's memo. He was sure there must be another story here. Leo shrugged his shoulders, put on his coat, and headed out for a much-needed drink.

Subtext

In order to penetrate to the heart of Clyde's memo, we must look for the subtext. Clyde is on a mission. From one perspective, his memo appears reasonable. Capital Success Training is making sound business decisions. Clyde is introducing policies to reduce costs and increase profits. Who could argue with that?

But take a look at the tone of Clyde's memo. Is it persuasive or domineering? If you were a trainer reading the memo, would you be angry and feel insulted by his tone? Clyde does not leave room for the trainers' reactions. He tries to anticipate their emotions and responds by slinging threats at them. Some examples of words or phrases used in this memo that threaten rather than represent shared thinking are, "I guess you are one of the trainers who hasn't been able or willing to sell" and "I'll miss working with you." Phrases such as these put distance between the writer and the readers and do little to engage a partnership for productivity.

Questions for Reflection

Before reading any further, take a few moments to think about the following questions:

1. What was your first reaction to the memo?
2. What is the sales manager's perspective? What is the trainer's perspective? What is the organizational perspective?
3. Can you imagine any alternative policies?
4. What can you deduce about this company? What would it be like to work there?

Analysis

There could be many stories behind Clyde's tone. Perhaps his boss is breathing down his neck to achieve better sales and profits. Clyde may believe his job is at stake if he doesn't increase the bottom line through sales. Clyde is a frightened bully. His story is out of control. Even his use of a tree metaphor is out of place.

One thing we can be sure of is that Clyde has lost his perspective and control. And while his tone and his failure to motivate trainers may be clear to others, Clyde himself is oblivious to all of the subtexts of his message. Clyde is locked into his story. Our capacity to actively listen to his story enables us to gain insights, but Clyde's inability to listen holds him prisoner.

Incidentally, Clyde's memo sheds light on Capital Success Training's story. What business are they really in? From the memo it appears that Capital Success is more interested in selling products than providing training. Maybe it's time for the company to rename itself Capital Success Resources and Lectures.

Vignette #6: House of Fashion

Gloria hesitated as she picked up the phone to call the House of Fashion customer service department. It was hard to believe she had been their loyal customer for over 30 years. In light of all the complications and poor customer service she had been receiving recently, Gloria found it difficult to stay focused on the positive experiences she had had with the company over the years.

Gloria's billing statements included charges totaling $2,005 that were not hers. She had been reassured many times that the charges would be removed. However, after five months, the charges were still on her statement. Now, Gloria had to call customer service with yet another issue, and she wasn't looking forward to the conversation. Gloria finished dialing the telephone number and hoped for the best.

Meanwhile, Jill, the newest member of the House of Fashion customer service department, began tackling a pile of unresolved customer issues. She wished she had never taken the job. Jill's mentor had persuaded her to work in customer service to gain a better understanding of the business and its customers. After several months of dealing with whiny, persnickety people all day, Jill found it hard to listen to customers' stories.

When the phone rang in Jill's office, she unenthusiastically picked it up and said, "Good morning. House of Fashion customer service department. This is Jill speaking."

"Good morning, Jill, this is Gloria Vera. I was hoping you could help me."

"I'll see what I can do," Jill tersely interjected. "What seems to be the problem?"

"I purchased a gown four months ago. It's gorgeous, and I have really enjoyed wearing it. Last week I took the gown to be dry cleaned, and when I got it back it was ripped in two places."

Before Gloria could finish her explanation, Jill interrupted. "Listen, Ms. Vera, House of Fashion cannot be responsible for damage done to your gown by a dry cleaner. I suggest you go back to the dry cleaner to resolve your problem."

"Jill, would you please let me finish? I have been using the same dry cleaner for 20 years, and I have never had any problems. On the few occasions when there has been a problem, my dry cleaner has always paid for any damage done to my clothes."

Jill answered in a very agitated tone." Gloria, we cannot be sure of your dry cleaner's work. Therefore, I'm afraid there is nothing I can do for you. I suggest you go back to them to resolve your problem."

"I have been a good customer for over 30 years," responded Gloria.

"I'm looking at your records and I see an outstanding balance of two thousand and five dollars," barked Jill. "Maybe your gown ripped while you were wearing it."

Gloria had reached the end of her patience. "Are you implying that I'm not being honest? You should do a little research before you start questioning my track record. Those charges are the result of errors and are being removed. If you scroll further down on your computer screen, you will see notes indicating the errors that have been made, as well as the corrective actions to be taken. You will see that I have been waiting five months for those charges to be removed from my statement.

"As far as the gown is concerned, I called to see if we could contact the manufacturer. The rips in the gown are most likely the result of poor material. Since it is clear you have no intention of listening to me or helping me, I will contact the manufacturer myself."

Gloria slammed the phone down and vowed to never again buy anything from House of Fashion. Incredulous, Jill looked at the phone. She wondered if she was ever going to understand customers.

Questions for Reflection

Before reading any further, take a few moments to think about the following questions:

1. Why can't Jill listen to Gloria?
2. Is it likely that Jill's customer service skills will improve?
3. How could she have better handled Gloria's call?

Analysis

Gloria is a victim of Jill's inability to listen. Preconceptions are the enemy of active listening. It is clear that Jill does not enjoy her job. Her disposition will immediately make it difficult for her to empathize with a customer. Jill is not open to encountering new perspectives because she has another story fixed in her mind. Jill's tone is defensive, and she demonstrates that she is incapable of listening to Gloria.

As Gloria tries to explain her situation, Jill keeps jumping to conclusions. In an effort to discount Gloria's story completely, Jill quickly looks up Gloria's account on her computer. However, in her hast, Jill does not look at all the information because she already thinks she knows what the story should be. Sadly, House of Fashion loses a customer, and it appears that Jill hasn't learned anything from her experience. Jill is locked into her story. Until she tries to listen actively, she will keep repeating the same story.

Vignette #7: The Math Riddle

It was a dreary New England day, and the last place I wanted to be was stuck in a cold, dirty waiting area of a car repair garage. I grabbed a magazine and settled into my chair. Because it was so early in the morning, there was only one other person in the large waiting area, and I selected a chair on the opposite end of the room from her. After a few minutes, an old man appeared with a bucket, squeegee, and some rags. He started cleaning the windows in a slow and deliberate manner. I gave a brief glance his way and then went back to my hermit-like behavior. He appeared content, focused on his task, and uninterested in interacting with anyone.

The young woman at the other end of the room began to fidget, and I could tell she was becoming uncomfortable. I looked in her direction and realized she felt uneasy watching the old man work. He did seem to be laboring a bit but nothing that warranted any special attention. I think she just didn't like being a passive spectator. It must have insulted her sensibilities to see someone else working and not make an effort to help him or at least acknowledge him. Her agitation reached a threshold and words came tumbling out of her mouth, "Good morning," she said, directing her salutations toward the old man.

Peering from the edge of my magazine, I observed the old man cock his head slightly but he did not reply. Determined to get a response, the woman repeated her greeting. Again, the old man ignored her.

Trying one last time she blurted out in operatic fashion, "How are you doing?" This time the old man turned around slowly facing her and in a deep rich Irish brogue said, "I have a question for you, missy. What's half of two plus two?" Oblivious to the man's clear irritation, she giggled and did not respond. So he pressed again, "Come on now, missy, it's a simple question, what's half of two plus two?"

She smiled and responded, "Two, of course." Sitting as an innocent spectator on the other end of the room, I began to wonder where this whole thing was going. He looked in my direction and said, "What about you, lad, what's half of two plus two?" Now math has never been one of my strong points, but I thought I could manage this one, so I answered, "two." He continued to press both of us, "Now I want you think real carefully, what's half of two, plus two?" He paused and then went in for the kill, "there's a reason why God gave you two ears and only one mouth."

Questions for Reflection

Before reading any further, take a few moments to think about the following questions:

1. In what ways does the woman fail to listen actively to the old man in the story?
2. What are some of the ways the old man's riddle functions?

Analysis

This is a true story. It is a wonderful miniexample of the same challenges faced by organizations. Some may accuse the man of poor communication by presenting a riddle. However, since the woman was preoccupied with her own feelings, she did not pay attention to the cues available to her. The story is a classic case of self-perceptions influencing communications. If she had been listening by being mindful of the situation, she would have never engaged the old man in conversation. Like the chatting woman, organizations need to focus more on listening and less on talking to communicate effectively.

The math riddle illustrates the interrelationship between listening, assumptions, and communication. Because we were predisposed to answer the riddle in a certain way, we were unable to see other possibilities. The power of the man's communication is not a function of chicanery. The fact that we answered the riddle wrong is not important. The man found an effective way to use a form of storytelling to ask us to leave him alone and be better listeners. His communication operated on multiple levels and gave me a lasting story to reflect on and share with others.

Vignette #8: The Spoon[1]

Once upon a time, there was an orphaned girl living with her cruel stepmother and stepsister. The poor girl slaved every day under the harsh and relentless scrutiny of her stepmother and incessant ridicule of her stepsister. One day the girl was down at the river washing silverware. One of the spoons slipped from her fingers and quickly sank to the depths far beyond her reach. As she fought back her tears, she noticed an old woman sunning herself on the rocks. The old woman called out to her, "What's the problem, sweetie?"

"I have lost one of mother's best silver spoons. She will never forgive me and will beat me for sure," the girl cried.

"Perhaps I can help you," responded the old woman. "But first will you come over here and scratch my back?"

The girl composed herself and began to climb across the rocks to reach the old woman. As she scratched the old woman's back, her hands were cut and torn by the woman's rough skin. Despite the discomfort, the girl continued to scratch the old woman's back. The woman turned to look at the girl and noticed how her hands were scraped. She quickly healed them by releasing a long slow exhale, breathing directly on the girl's hands. Then the old woman said to the girl, "Before I help you recover your spoon, please come to my home for a meal."

The girl agreed and the two set off to the old woman's home. The woman took a huge pot and handed it to the girl, saying, "Let's make a scrumptious soup. Fill the pot with water, place this single bean in the water along with this bone, add a grain of rice, and we will have a feast."

The girl looked incredulously at the old woman, but she could sense her earnest conviction. Pushing aside her doubts, the girl did as the old woman had instructed. When the soup was done, the two sat down to a splendid meal. It was the most wonderful soup the girl had ever tasted. When the meal was over the old woman turned to the girl and said, "I need to go out for a little bit; stay here and when I return we will recover your spoon. While I am out,

1. Reprinted with permission from M. E. Sharpe, Armonk, New York—*The Strategic Use of Stories in Organizational Communication and Learning,* Terrence L. Gargiulo © 2005.

if a black cat comes by, you mustn't feed him no matter how much he meows. Beat him with this broom." The girl nodded and the old woman left.

After a little while, a black cat wandered into the house and began meowing loudly. The girl glanced at the cat and at first tried to ignore him but before too long the girl took some leftovers from lunch and fed the cat. When the old woman returned, she was noticeably very happy and said to the girl, "You are so kind and helpful, why don't you stay with me a little while?"

Although tempted by the offer, the girl responded, "I would love to but I must get back to my stepmother and stepsister. Would you please tell me how I can recover the spoon I lost?"

"As you walk home," started the old woman, "you will come to a crossroads. You will see a pile of eggs. There will be large ones shouting out to you: 'Take me, take me!' Among the eggs there will be some tiny ones saying nothing. Take one of the tiny eggs and break it open when you reach the next crossroad."

The girl hugged the old woman, thanked her for her hospitality, and set out. Just as the old woman had described, when the girl got to the first crossroad she saw a pile of eggs. Unperturbed by the large eggs' incessant cries of "Take me, take me," the girl searched for the tiniest egg she could find. When she got to the next crossroad, per the old woman's instructions, she cracked open the egg. To her utter surprise, a magnificent golden chest grew in front of her eyes, and inside were hundreds of spoons, knives, and forks made of the finest silver. When she returned home with her treasure, the girl's stepmother and stepsister were seized with jealousy. They insisted that she reveal to them how she acquired such a treasure.

The next day, the girl's stepmother sent her own daughter to the river to wash some silverware. When the girl got to the river she threw in a spoon. Without much of an effort to recover it, the girl began to cry in a loud voice. Once again there was an old woman sunning herself on the rocks. The old woman called out to her, "What's the problem, sweetie?"

"I have lost one of mother's best silver spoons. She will never forgive me and will beat me for sure," the girl cried.

"Perhaps I can help you," responded the woman. "But first will you come over here and scratch my back?"

The girl climbed across the rocks to reach the old woman and began to scratch her back. Suddenly she shrieked. "What's the matter?" asked the old woman.

"Your back is disgusting and it is cutting my hands and making them bleed."

The old woman healed the girl's hand by releasing a long slow exhale and directing it on the girl's hands. Then the old woman said to her, "Before I help you recover your spoon, please come to my home for a meal."

The girl agreed and the two set off to the old woman's home. She took a huge pot and handed it to the girl, saying, "Let's make a scrumptious soup. Fill the pot with water, place this single bean in the water along with this bone and a grain of rice, and we will have a feast."

"You have to be kidding. This will make a vile soup," said the girl.

"Mind your tongue and do as I have asked," responded the old woman.

Soon after, a delectable stew brimming with rice and beans was ready and the two ate their meal in silence. When the meal was over, the old woman turned to the girl and said, "I need to go out for a little bit, stay here and when I return we will recover your spoon. While I am out, if a black cat comes by, you mustn't feed him no matter how much he meows. Beat him with this broom." The girl nodded and the old woman left.

After a little while, a black cat wandered into the house and began meowing loudly. Immediately the girl picked up the broom and began beating the cat senselessly until she broke one of its legs. The cat managed to hobble away. Later that evening the old woman came home leaning on a cane because one of her legs was broken. She instructed the girl to leave her house.

The girl reminded the old woman that she could not go home without her silver spoon. "As you walk home," started the old woman, "you will come to a crossroad. You will see a pile of eggs. There will be large ones shouting out to you: 'Take me, take me!' Among the eggs there will be some tiny ones saying nothing. Take one of the tiny eggs and break it open when you reach the next crossroad."

Without a word of thanks, the girl ran out of the house. When she got to the first crossroad she saw a pile of eggs. The large ones all yelled, "Take me, take me!"

"I am not naïve," the girl thought to herself. "I will listen to what these eggs are telling me." She picked out the biggest egg and broke it right where she was standing. Instantly, a horde of dragons, demons, and devils appeared and ate the girl.

Questions for Reflection

Before reading any further, take a few moments to think about the following questions:

1. How do the two girls react differently to the old woman's instructions?
2. What guides each girl's actions in the story?

Analysis

This marvelous story is one of my favorite folk tales. On the surface, it may seem like the story is more about trust and following instructions than about active listening. However, these are essential aspects of active listening. The first girl trusts herself to decide when to follow the woman's instructions. Her listening involves reflection. She is not entirely obedient. Each instruction given to her by the woman is processed individually. She listens as much to herself as to the woman. The second girl, on the other hand, is blinded by greed. Her internal dialogue is dominated by a preoccupation of acquiring the treasure discovered by the first girl. She is incapable of listening actively.

STORIES HELP US NEGOTIATE DIFFERENCES

Communication is the foundation for managing. There is no communication without active listening. Stories are wonderful vehicles for increasing our capacity for active listening. As evidenced by the collection of vignettes above, active listening takes on many different forms. Active listening is at the heart of our work with stories. With active listening, it becomes possible to negotiate our differences because we are prepared to deeply hear one another and learn from our different perspectives.

Conflicts in organizations are the result of clashing points of view. Of course people have different points of view, but consider some of the dichotomies that naturally exist in organizations. For example, there is usually competition between sales and marketing, product development and marketing, or tensions between labor and management. Each functional area has its own organizational perspective and its own turf to protect. Often the interests of management are not in sync with the desires and needs of labor. Managers are challenged to consider each perspective while negotiating the differences between them.

When negotiating differences in either a conflict or decision-making process, it is essential to hear, appreciate, understand, and acknowledge all of the perspectives. Stories are a quick way to gain important insights. We are inclined to rationally explain and justify our perspectives; however, there are always experiences, values, and beliefs behind perspectives. Stories shed light on these experiences, values, and beliefs and can reveal a host of hard-to-identify motivations, such as fear and self-interest. Stories get to the heart of matters and help us imagine other perspectives.

What's inherently difficult about negotiating differences is that when faced with two strong points of view, opinions, or ideas, there is always some validity to each of them. This can be paralyzing. If each point of view has some validity, how do you draw a fair conclusion? Think about how a trial works. Each side presents its story. A jury must work through each side of the story. In the end, the jury synthesizes all of the information and formulates a story of its own to make a decision.

Using stories as a way of negotiating differences or getting to the root cause of a problem works because, unlike reasoning, stories are not linear. Although the sequence of events in a story follows a logical order, the themes and messages contained in it allow our minds to entertain paradoxes. Through stories we can simultaneously hold multiple and conflicting points of view as being true and consider them all without one negating the other. This leads to a very rich experience, because our minds must open to a whole world of nuances.

When we actively listen to stories, we are invited to enter a novel frame of reference. The story provides us with the material to work emotionally and logically with new information. Placing two or more viewpoints side by side presents an opportunity to imagine a whole new set of possibilities previously hidden. The stories provide a safe and often depersonalized sandbox in which to work out our differences.

Arbitrators are excellent at helping people to consider conflicting points of view. There is a direct correlation between the success of a mutually satisfying outcome in arbitration and the degree to which people share and hear each other's stories. Like arbitrators, managers can increase their effectiveness at negotiating differences by setting aside time and a safe space for people to tell their stories. Managers must use the experiences of people shared in the form of stories to engage them in conversations full of rich exchanges. The stories become participatory theaters in which clashing ideas and competing desires and needs can be played out.

Vignette #9: Joe versus Jane

Joe Employee and Jane Manager are having problems. Joe is furious with Jane because she will not give him funds to hire an outside consultant to help with a project. Initially, Jane had promised him all of the resources he would need. The project was a top priority. Jane had selected Joe to head it because of his proven ability to deliver. Jane had also recognized that outside help would be necessary in order to complete the project. Joe took on the project in good faith, understanding that he would be able to hire consultants. When the situation suddenly changed and Joe could not hire outside consultants, he took it personally. He believes Jane is setting him up for failure. Joe starts going out of his way to criticize Jane, and he lets other projects slip through the cracks.

Due to new management, Jane's budget was cut by more than 30 percent in the middle of the year. Management appears to have new priorities but has not been clear with Jane about the direction to be taken. Jane is experiencing a lot of pressure and uncertainty. She is doing her best to get through all the chaos. She is frustrated that Joe, one of her best and most loyal employees, is being difficult. Jane becomes cross with him at meetings and starts to cut back on other resources that Joe needs.

Questions for Reflection

Before reading any further, take a few moments to think about the following questions:

1. How has each person contributed to this situation spiraling out of control?
2. What could each person do differently?
3. What role could stories play in negotiating differences between Joe and Jane?

Analysis

One of the main causes of conflict is a breakdown of communication. Communication always breaks down when one person cannot see another person's perspective. Understanding another person's point of view often means suspending one's own. We do not like to abandon our perspective; doing so can be very disorienting. So, entering into a conflict actually becomes the path of least resistance. It does not take much energy to start a conflict. Yet, ironically, holding on to negative feelings takes more energy than resolving a conflict. Negative perceptions can even drive future destructive behavior, and things can quickly spiral out of control.

Your job is to be a story facilitator. Joe and Jane need to tell their stories. You need to help develop each story and help the two see each other's perspective. Active listening will play a major role. Joe needs to see how he became wrapped up in the project and inattentive to Jane and her situation. He will have to recognize how his zeal for the project affected his behavior and attitude. Perhaps Jane had always been a good communicator, but the current pressures made it difficult for her. She may also have been waiting for clearer information from management. Jane will need to see how seriously Joe has taken the project and how disillusioned he became when he was unable to complete it. Despite the lack of information and the company's conservative management style, Jane needs to acknowledge the impact on Joe of her poor communication.

Vignette #10: Charlie's Dilemma

Charlie's 30 years at the company had to count for something. He paced back and forth in the waiting area. He was not interested in becoming another statistic. The new management team needed to hear what he had to say.

The door of the office opened and one of Charlie's closest colleagues walked out with a long face. He was shaking his head and barely noticed Charlie standing outside the office. Charlie stopped his colleague, who managed to mumble under his breath, "it's waste of time, Charlie, these kids just don't get it."

A voice from inside the office called out, "Come in, Charlie, take a seat."

Seated behind the desk were two of the company's youngest and finest new managers. Polly and Dan were graduates of the best business school in the country. They came with a long list of credentials, but as far as Charlie was concerned they lacked the requisite knowledge of the business and its market to be such influential decision makers in the company. Polly and Dan assumed senior-level leadership positions two months ago, and since then, more 20 people had been laid off. Ironically, the company was profitable.

Charlie supervised a team of 15 men on the factory floor. For the last five years his team had been among the top performers in the company, breaking all of the production records. Charlie walked into the office and slumped into the chair in front of the desk.

"Thanks for coming, Charlie," said Dan. "You and your team have an impressive track record. I'm sure it comes as no surprise to you that the company must reduce the expenses of excessive production to maximize our profit margins to be in line with analysts' expectations. Consequently, we have been asked by the executive team to find opportunities for cost cutting. Your team's production is creating over-capacity that is eating away at the company's bottom line. Our analysis indicates that a team of 10 would be more than adequate to meet our production schedule. We have taken a preliminary look at the performance of members of your team and have come up with some recommendations on who we think you can let go. Of course, it's your team and you're free to right-size the team as you see fit, but you may find this report helpful. We'll need your final decision on who we will be laying off no later than next Friday. Polly is working with HR to put together some attractive packages. We will have the details to you on Monday. Sorry for the bad news. You are a great asset to the company, and, on behalf of the executive team, I want to thank you for helping to make this company a success. If you have any questions, feel free to drop me an e-mail."

Charlie was stunned and for a moment did not even move in his chair. He did not know what to say; and even if he did, he wasn't so sure Polly and Dan would be interested in hearing it.

Questions for Reflection

Before reading any further, take a few moments to think about the following questions:

1. Even though you do not have all the information, how would you coach Polly and Dan to handle their conversation with Charlie?
2. How would you coach Charlie to respond?
3. Can you imagine any other outcomes to this meeting?

Analysis

We've all seen or heard about this type of meeting. It's the didactic tone that is completely ineffectual. There are no stories being exchanged. Sometimes the shortest distance between two points of view is a circuitous route. On the surface, stories may seem indirect, slow, or even cumbersome, especially in a delicate situation like the one portrayed in the vignette. It might be hard to imagine how stories will help, but look at the effect of Polly's and Dan's no-nonsense approach.. They are polite, professional, courteous, and even acknowledge Charlie's contributions. So what's wrong? There's no genuine conversation, there's no vulnerability, and there are no stories. All in all, this is an excellent example of poor communication and abominable management.

Putting aside the unknown details of the situation, let's imagine how Polly, Dan, and Charlie might use stories to negotiate differences. First, the physical setting of the room needs to be changed. People facing each other across a desk is not an arrangement that is conducive to the openness required by stories. Second, Polly and Dan could begin the session by asking a few questions. Charlie probably has some preconceived ideas about the nature of the meeting. They should give him a chance to discuss what he has heard. Whatever impressions Charlie has about the reasons for the meeting and the company's current state of affairs are part of a core story that will influence his future perceptions and impact his behaviors. Polly and Dan must elicit these fragments of information to understand where Charlie is coming from. Some of the stories he has heard will have validity and others will not. Polly and Dan can navigate these nuances once they have more information.

Next Polly and Dan should share a short story or two of their own. These stories would serve two purposes. First, if the stories are told with authenticity, they will begin to create an environment of trust. The stories will act as an invitation. When trust is established, the appropriate response to a story is to tell one. Polly and Dan want to elicit Charlie's experiences in the form of stories. Second, the stories can transmit important details and perspectives that Charlie might not be aware of. In all likelihood, Charlie has not looked at the situation from Polly's and Dan's perspective and he probably hasn't considered the company's perspective.

There may be no silver lining in the situation, but at the very least people feel heard and understood. It's important to realize that using stories to negotiate differences does not mean everyone can be satisfied. In the case of this vignette, Polly, Dan, and Charlie may not have any control over the company's strategy or directives. On the other hand, managing complex communications with stories can yield some surprising results. The stories produce new fertile ground for breakthrough solutions and options.

SUMMARY

Active listening is at the heart of what makes storytelling such a powerful tool for managers. Through active listening, managers can quickly get to the essence of situations, discover the root cause of problems, and honestly assess their biases. Effective leaders know how to enter new frames of reference in order to see things from other people's perspectives. Stories also allow them to hold diverse points of view and negotiate differences without abnegating their own.

4 / *Case Study—Sodexho*

THE PREVIOUS CHAPTER explored two essential communication functions of stories: stories require active listening, and stories help negotiate differences. This chapter provides an example of how these two functions can be applied at an organizational level.

Some organizations are becoming more mindful and purposeful in how they use stories. The organizations I have been working with have gone beyond the obvious communication applications and have discovered ways to make stories a central part of new management practices. Stories are prominent in discussions about how to transform the cultures of their organizations. These companies start by listening to stories from their employees and customers and, in the process, realize a whole new way of thinking about themselves.

One of the most gratifying aspects of my work with organizations is helping them find their magic. The pervasive grind of employees' day-to-day roles and responsibilities tends to erode their appreciation of what makes their organization special. The simple act of making time for people to share their organizational stories and encouraging them to listen actively yields tremendous results in employees' level of engagement and excitement. As the stories are told, a tapestry of key stories emerges. These stories define the company's strengths and become central beacons of purpose and volition. There are additional benefits of informal learning. As the stories spread through the organization, they produce new networks of learning and information exchange that might otherwise remain dormant or undiscovered.

A good way to jumpstart the process is to ask employees share customer stories. Starbucks Coffee begins almost every internal meeting with a customer story—so simple, yet so powerful. Once a climate of story sharing exists and people are listening actively to one another, it becomes more possible to negotiate differences and leverage the diversity of perspectives, talents, and organizational strengths for future success. Below is a case study discussing how Sodexho has begun to introduce stories into its management practices.

SODEXHO AND STORIES

The following section was written by Angelo Ioffreda, vice president of internal communications at Sodexho.

Background

Sodexho is the leading provider of food and facilities management in the United States and offers innovative outsourcing solutions in food service, housekeeping, grounds keeping, plant operations and maintenance, asset management, and laundry services to more than 6,000 corporations, health care, long-term care and retirement centers, schools, college campuses, and military and remote sites in North America.

Sodexho is integrating storytelling into its workplace with several objectives in mind: (1) to obtain feedback from employees and insight into the company's culture, and (2) to hone our brand and employee value proposition, and (3) to share the positive experiences of working at Sodexho to raise morale and instill company pride.

As part of our management and communication strategies involving stories, Sodexho launched an essay contest in July 2004. We sent out a flyer in English and Spanish that was e-mailed to all of our managers. The topic of the essay contest was, "what I like best about my job at Sodexho." Stories were accepted in English, Spanish, and French and we profiled the winners in the company magazine, *Solutions*.

Selection Process

Sodexho selected the top stories on the basis of how well they expressed the essence and individual experience of working for Sodexho. We received 74 essays. From these, we selected five winners, each of whom received a $100 gift certificate. Four of these winners were profiled in the January 2005 issue of the company magazine. In addition, five honorable mention winners each received a $50 gift certificate. The top ten essays were sent with a cover note via e-mail to all managers, and all the essays were posted on the company intranet site.

Sodexho's "Tell Us Your Story" Contest

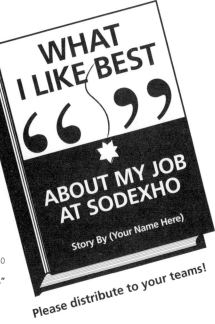

We're pleased to announce **Sodexho's "Tell Us Your Story" contest open to all Sodexho employees** in the United States and Canada.

To Enter:

Employees should submit a story of no more than 250 words by 5:00 PM Eastern time on August 16th on the topic of: **"What I like best about my job at Sodexho."** Stories will be accepted in English, Spanish and French.

Entrants should include their:

- Name
- Position
- Unit name
- Business line or department
- Address
- Phone number
- e-mail address

Selecting the Winners

Five great stories will be selected on the basis of **how well they express the essence and individual experience of working for Sodexho**. Each winner will receive a **$100 American Express gift certificate**. Winning stories will be posted on SodexhoNet. We will announce the winners on September 3rd.

Submitting your story:

Stories can be sent in via one of the following methods **by 5:00 PM on August 16th**.

e-mail:

SodexhoEssayContest@sodexhousa.com
fax: 1.301.987.4438

mail:

Sodexho's "Tell Us Your Story" Contest
c/o Corporate Communications
9801 Washingtonian Blvd., Suite 1218
Gaithersburg, MD 20878

If you have any questions about this contest, please call 1.301.987.4320

El concurso de Sodexho: "Cuéntanos tu historia"

Con gran orgullo, les presentamos **el concurso "Cuéntanos tu historia." Todos los empleados de Sodexho** del Canadá y los Estados Unidos pueden participar.

Para Participar:

Empleados deben de someter una historia de menos de 250 palabras y entregarla antes de las 5:00 de la tarde, hora del este, del 16 de agosto. El tema del concurso es: **"Lo que más me gusta de mi trabajo con Sodexho."** Vamos a aceptar historias en inglés, español y francés.

Los participantes deben incluir la siguiente información:

- Nombre.
- Puesto.
- Nombre de su unidad.
- Línea de negocio o departamento en el que trabaja.
- Dirección.
- Número de teléfono.
- Dirección electrónica o de e-mail.

Proceso de selección de ganadores

Vamos a elegir cinco fabulosas historias, **las que mejor expresen la esencia de la experiencia de cada individuo en su trabajo con Sodexho.** Cada ganador, o ganadora, recibirá **$100 dólares americanos en un certificado para regalo Express.** Las historias ganadoras se podrán leer en el sitio SodexhoNet. Anunciaremos los nombres de los ganadores el 3 de septiembre.

Para someter su historia:

Puede usar cualquiera de los siguientes métodos para someter su historia **antes de las 5:00 de la tarde del 16 de agosto.**

Envíela a la dirección electrónica:

SodexhoEssayContest@sodexhousa.com
fax: 1.301.987.4438

Correo:
Si decide enviar su historia por correo, envíela a la siguiente dirección:

**Sodexho's "Tell Us Your Story" Contest
c/o Corporate Communications
9801 Washingtonian Blvd., Suite 1218
Gaithersburg, MD 20878**

Si tiene alguna pregunta en cuanto al concurso, por favor llámenos al: 1-301-987-4320

Sometiendo una historia, usted concede qué elenvía será juzgado no-confidencial yconcede a Sodexho la derecha de utilizar, copiar, modificar, corregir, publicar, transmitir y exhibir su sumisión vía cualquier medio, y que Sodexho estará libre deutilizar su nombre y la otra información que identifica, a menos que usted solicite específicamente en la escritura queno tenemos el derecho.

Optimizing Use of the Stories

The stories were compelling and provided great insight into Sodexho. Our goal was to give these stories broad exposure and to optimize their use. The company's follow-up included:

- E-mailing winning stories to all managers.
- Posting all essays on our intranet and communicating this.
- Preparing a summary report of main themes from these stories and sending this to the executive team, the human resources department, and the company's communicators. Among the findings of the report:
  - o Our mission and values resonate with employees.
  - o Employees are proud of our company and some of its specific initiatives.
  - o The opportunity Sodexho provides for employees' personal and professional improvement is very important.
  - o The people make all the difference. Many stories recounted the understanding, care, and support of managers, colleagues, and peers, especially in difficult situations such as personal or family illness.
  - o Employees feel the company cares about them and treats them well.

- Preparing a presentation that was shown at our annual management conference that highlighted excerpts from various essays.
- Developing an article for the company magazine.

Impact

We received positive feedback on the essays and look forward to additional feedback after the stories are published. According to an internal communications survey, 95 percent of employees reported high morale and pride in the company and its work. The impact of this storytelling experiment, while significant when the essays were shared, has been limited. However, the stage has been set for storytelling (and contests to elicit input) as part of the way Sodexho does business.

Here are a few of the comments from those who read the essays:

I just finished reading the winning essays. All were inspiring and some were very heartwarming. I hope you'll run the contest again as an annual event. Have a good holiday weekend.

—Sodexho manager

WOW! Thanks for sharing these remarkable essays.

—human resources manager

That's powerful stuff and beautifully presented!

—technical writer

Sample Stories from the Essay Contest

Lisa K. Hart
Sales Coordinator, Campus Services
Altamonte Springs, Florida

Sodexho is a wonderful organization to work for and has helped me throughout a very difficult time in my life. In January 2003, I was diagnosed with stage three cancer. I approached my supervisor at Sodexho in quite an emotional state, and she was supportive and steady. She helped me deal with my personal crisis in a professional and kindly way, while at the same time making certain the company did not suffer.

I underwent over a year of extensive treatments, during which I had to take a leave of absence. During my entire leave, Sodexho was there for me—keeping in touch, sending flowers when I was hospitalized, mailing cards, sending e-mails, and even preparing nutritional and delicious individual meals and bringing them to my home! I never had to worry about health insurance or disability benefits, because being a Sodexho employee enabled me to have what I needed. All of this was a blessing during this difficult time.

As of March of this year, I was declared cancer-free and able to return to work. Once again, Sodexho was supportive and worked hard to accommodate a reduced work schedule, changing my job assignment, and making sure I was able to continue to work while I also continued to heal.

I'm much better now, and, God willing, well on the road to recovery. Without Sodexho's support, I doubt I would have gotten this far. I am truly grateful that I work for such an outstanding organization, filled with people who care about the person, not just the employee.

Jewel Henkes
Cashier, United Airlines Headquarters
Arlington Heights, Illinois

What's not to like about my position as a cashier with Sodexho at United Airlines headquarters? I meet and chat with people worldwide, and my mind certainly has been expanded by comments about my own nation from the point of view of clientele who have experienced life in other countries. And what would I do without the other Sodexho employees whom I work with? I think we work well together, having fun at the same time while serving our clientele.

It seems employees like to use me as a way to clear their minds, to let go of the pressure demanded by their jobs, and most of the employees know me by name. Sometimes clientele are transferred and when they return here a few years later, we immediately recognize each other and there are hugs all around. I can't even find the words to describe these reunions, but this is one of the reasons my job with Sodexho is so memorable. I have been employed with Sodexho for more than seven years and I have had so much fun I would not trade this for anything else. I will be 77 years old on September 13, and employment here has made my later life rewarding.

I would like to work with Sodexho a few more years because I enjoy the work, and I would like to visit other countries like Australia, Japan, and Russia. Two years ago, I flew to Germany and learned quite a bit.

Ramona Moton
Catering, Youngstown University
Youngstown, Ohio

My name is Ramona Moton. I am a recovering alcoholic/addict, grandmother and mother, and a born-again Christian. When I came to Youngstown University (a Sodexho account) I was still living in a halfway house. I thought finding a job would be impossible. I learned soon enough, all things are possible. I was hired in working utility, which consisted of mopping floors and emptying trash, which wasn't enough for me. Because of my hard work, determination, and pride, my work ethic did not go unnoticed. I soon was promoted with a raise. With excellent training, I learned to do every job in the food court. I now work catering, which for me was one of the most challenging positions I've experienced.

Sodexho has given me a new way of life. It has taught me that if you work hard, there's nothing you can't accomplish. I now am considering taking some classes, after 25 years of being out of school. Everyone here gives 110 percent of themselves no matter how long or tedious their jobs. I've never met so many hard-working team-playing professionals. I've learned that for things to run smoothly, you have to have fair but tough administrators. They expect the best because that's what they give.

I would like to thank the staff, administration, supervisors, cooks, and fellow employees for making what could be a hard job easy. I know that things sometimes can get stressful, but working with supportive considerate, family-like peers, we can do a job and know that it reflects on what Sodexho stands for: pride.

Mahmoud M. Na'amneh
Caterer, University of California, Davis
Davis, California

I still remember my first day of work at Sodexho as if it were yesterday, even though it has been five years now. The first task assigned to me was to clean the bathroom, a task that I had never done before, but one that would change my life forever. Reluctantly, I accepted the task and hastily I finished it. I could hear the echo of my deep sigh as I flushed down my self-esteem. I went home and immediately rushed to the shower to purify my body and soul.

But wait, I did not really give up, as I am not a quitter. I went back to work with determination to excel and overachieve. I stripped the "culture of shame" that I carried with me when I came to the United States five years ago. I grew up in Jordan, where men are not supposed to clean bathrooms or wash dishes. I felt that I was reborn, and Sodexho was the midwife that orchestrated this birth. Cleaning the bathroom was a rite of passage to my renewed self and soul.

I continued to work as a dishwasher at Sodexho and a teaching assistant at the anthropology department at UC Davis. What a nice combination! Believe me, I created a nice synthesis between them and I loved both jobs equally. I was then promoted to be a caterer, my current position. I sometimes serve my students and I always take pride in so doing.

Sodexho is not just a workplace. It is indeed a small family that functions as an agent of socialization. Determination, good ethics, teamwork, and believing in oneself will be the eternal legacy of Sodexho in my life.

SUMMARY

During a follow-up interview, Lyn Adame, director of communications of Sodexho's health care division, shared with me some interesting information on the emerging role of stories in Sodexho's culture. She recounted how her quarterly magazine, *Team Connections,* has become a place to collect success stories and share best practices. However, given the communication challenge of reaching so many employees and the infrequent nature of the publication, she realized it wasn't enough. So she began an initiative called "Sodexho Smile." In support of the health care division's new branding effort to put clients' needs first and at the heart of everyone's work, this initiative encourages employees to share their stories of "making a difference" and "point of pride stories," informally, up and down the organization, and all of the time. Employees look forward to sharing on a daily basis their stories about how they have made a difference. For example, there was a story of a long-term child patient who, at the last minute, decided he wanted to attend a Halloween party and dress up as a chef. Despite being swamped with her regular job responsibilities, a Sodexho employee stopped what she was doing to put together the patient's costume.

Lyn describes it this way: "We want our employees to feel emotional connectivity with the people they serve. It's all about having the right emotion at the right time and balancing that with the need to complete all of the demanding tasks that are part of their core job responsibilities. We are supporting Sodexho's core mission by being attuned to the needs of our customers."

Lyn and Angelo are not alone at Sodexho in believing that the practice of daily story sharing and "emotional connectivity" can positively change an organization's management culture. People's sense of the organization's mission will be vitalized by the ongoing exchange of experiences shared as narratives throughout the organization. The organization's vision includes helping its people find new ways of serving customers and talking about them. The seemingly superficial, extraneous activities that frequently go unnoticed throughout the organization start moving through the social fabric and create long-lasting results. The most amazing things about these results are that they are self-sustaining and self-perpetuating by virtue of their decentralized nature and by virtue of the medium through which they are shared: stories. And, as we learned in the last chapter, stories require active listening, and when we listen actively to one another and ourselves we begin connecting on a deeper and more fundamental level. So emotional connectivity can be naturally inculcated into an organization's culture by encouraging people to share their stories and listen actively to each other. Sodexho and many other organizations are pursuing this strategy and achieving amazing business and interpersonal results.

5 / *Leading through Stories*

RELATIONSHIPS ARE THE most important part of any leader's job. Communication, rapport, and what Daniel Goleman has coined as "emotional intelligence" are essential competencies that today's organizational leaders need to develop. In all areas of life, maintaining healthy relationships is the toughest work we ever do. Many people have a bad habit of assuming that relationships take care of themselves. We tend to think of relationships like mythical perpetual motion machines that require no ongoing energy to maintain their work. By their very nature, relationships are doomed to fail unless the participants are completely vested in them and work at them constantly. I am always surprised when I meet leaders who view their relationships as a burden. It is dangerous to become overly focused on what needs to be done and forget to nurture the relationships around us. All the other talents of leaders are reduced to a fraction of their potential when relationships are pushed to the sidelines.

This chapter examines two more functions of stories that are central to relationships: Stories help people bond with one another, and they promote healing. Although leaders should focus their energies in using stories for healing and in other positive ways, we will also look at how stories can be used as weapons.

STORIES HELP PEOPLE BOND WITH ONE ANOTHER

Stories allow people to bind to and bond with one another. First, let's define "bind" and "bond." Look carefully at this book. How is it held together? What makes the pages adhere to one another and bind to the spine of the book? Is there some glue holding all the pieces together?

Stories provide the same sort of glue between people. In other words, stories show how our experiences, memories, hopes, fears, and desires match with other persons'. I will be able to understand you and communicate effectively with you only when I am able to relate my stories to your stories. We must learn how to treat each person as a treasure chest waiting to be opened so that stories can enrich our experiences of others and enable us to build strong relationships.

In almost any situation, the shortest distance between two people is a story. Sales professionals discover early in their careers the importance of uncovering common linkages between themselves and potential customers. As humans, we thrive on these connections. No one likes to feel isolated. Stories act as bridges between our experiences. Through stories, people find common ground. Because stories require active listening, people can share a depth of experiences that would be otherwise impossible through normal dialogue. Stories can emphasize shades of meaning and feelings often left hidden or inadequately expressed in didactic forms of communication. As one person shares a story, the listener finds a similar correspondence from his or her experience.

Leaders must realize that an essential part of their job is to initiate connections between themselves and others, and among those inside and outside the organization. Christopher Locke and his colleagues in the groundbreaking work *The Cluetrain Manifesto: The End of Business as Usual,* demonstrate that the boundaries around organizations that separate the inside from the outside are very porous. The only way to communicate effectively and reliably inside and outside and across all of the elaborate interconnected nodes of communication is through stories.

Stories facilitate the development of bonds between people, thereby maximizing informal channels of communication. As people relate in overlapping and crisscrossing patterns with one another, leaders can leverage these relationships to move information, manage change, promote new understandings, encourage people to take ownership of the organization's success, and catalyze action. For leaders strategically focused on the critical nature of relationships, the capacity of stories to help people bond is one of the greatest tools they have at their disposal.

Most leaders should spend more time communicating informally to increase bonding occurrences. During these informal exchanges, leaders need to be mindful of what stories they tell. Their primary reason for telling stories should be to elicit them from others. Creating linkages between stories from inside and outside the organization is essential for building good relationships.

Vignette #11: Stuck on a Plane

Mitsu glanced at her watch for the umpteenth time and sighed. It was 6:32 P.M. Travel has become such a nuisance, she thought. Mitsu had been trying to get from New York to Boston since 8:00 A.M. She had been stuck in her seat for four hours, waiting for her plane to be cleared for takeoff.

Two seats away from her, Arlene was finding it increasingly difficult to sit still. All she could think about was Robert's violin recital. In less than an hour and a half, her son would be at Thatcher Elementary School giving his first recital, and she was not going to be there to hear it. Arlene struggled with pangs of guilt. She had never imagined that being both a mother and a professional would be so difficult. Arlene felt pulled in so many different directions. Worst of all, she felt completely powerless. And at the moment, there was nothing she could do but wait.

In a fit of frustration, Mitsu tossed her file of work down on the empty seat that separated her and Arlene. She reached inside her briefcase for a magazine. I should have stayed in New York this evening to see *Madame Butterfly* at the Metropolitan Opera, she thought to herself. Arlene's eyes caught the glossy cover of Mitsu's *Opera News* magazine. Not normally being one to speak to strangers on airplanes, she suddenly found herself directing a question toward Mitsu. "Are you an opera aficionado?" asked Arlene.

Mitsu blushed self-consciously, but answered with a warm smile, "I am more like a music junkie." Both women enjoyed a laugh. "Actually, being the daughter of a symphony and opera conductor, I have lived and breathed music my entire life."

"Then you must be a musician," Arlene said.

Mitsu tilted her head back slightly and paused a moment before answering. "Oddly enough, I am not a musician. Music plays a prominent role in my life, but I practice corporate law to pay the bills. My children laugh at me all the time. They find it ironic that their mother scrutinizes the minute details of contracts looking for legal loopholes by day, and emotes with Puccini and Verdi by night. My kids can always tell what kind of day I've had by the music I play. My oldest son, Brian, who is 16 and quite a pianist, bought me a pair of headphones for my birthday last year so I don't interrupt him while he's doing his homework."

Arlene broke eye contact with Mitsu and glanced at the floor. "I am going to miss my son's first violin recital this evening. I am a lawyer also, but I am finding it hard to balance my career with my family life." Arlene lifted her eyes from the floor and searched Mitsu's face, which was considerably older than her own, and asked, "How have you managed to be both a mother and a lawyer?"

Mitsu squinted her eyes thoughtfully and began to answer Arlene's question.

"Well… ."

Questions for Reflection

Before reading any further, take a few moments to think about the following questions:

1. What are the ways in which stories help form a bond between Mitsu and Arlene?
2. What role would stories play in the rest of this vignette if it continued?

Analysis

We see two travelers caught in an exasperating situation of flight delays. Each of them is focused in her own world. Mitsu tries to escape the situation by halting her work and enjoying an opera magazine. Arlene, on the other hand, is fixated on missing her son's first violin recital. When Arlene's eye catches the cover of Mitsu's music magazine, she feels impelled to speak. Mitsu responds to Arlene's question with a "warm smile" and a little humor. The humor eases the tension of the travel situation and breaks the awkwardness between two strangers communicating for the first time. If Mitsu had responded coldly, or more pedantically, the conversation may never have gone further.

Mitsu goes on to share a piece of personal information about herself. She reveals that her father was a conductor. Arlene is intrigued; she wants to know more about Mitsu and probes deeper by posing another question. Mitsu recognizes Arlene's interest and sees Arlene's question as an invitation to share more about herself. Mitsu seizes the opportunity and tells Arlene a story.

In a few sentences, Mitsu paints a vivid image of her life as a music aficionado, lawyer, and mother. Arlene listens intently. She sees similarities between Mitsu's life and her own professional and family situations. The two women connect with one another. Confident of the common glue between them, Arlene shares with Mitsu her doubts and fears about being both a mother and lawyer. Hungry for more stories, Arlene asks Mitsu to share her experiences.

This is not an uncommon occurrence. Strangers on a plane who strike up good conversations usually share lots of stories. Conversation based on an exchange of facts between strangers rarely goes on for any length of time. The first instance of story in this vignette is the cover of the *Opera News* magazine. Because Arlene is involved in her internal dialogue about her son's recital, the cover of Mitsu's magazine offers Arlene a way to externalize her feelings. Notice the rapid nature of stories in the vignette. Some of the stories are only one sentence, but they are still rich enough to pique the imaginations of Arlene and Mitsu and fuel their bonding.

Vignette #12: Scuba Leonard

Leonard scowled as he pinned his name badge to his jacket. Why did his boss insist that everyone attend these training sessions? They were always the same, and rarely did Leonard get much out of them. As he found a seat in the back of the room, all he could think about was the pile of work on his desk. He hoped his gruff disposition would discourage anyone from sitting next to him.

One of the things Leonard dreaded most about these training sessions was the cursory self-introductions. Instructors should realize that everyone already knew everybody they needed to know. Leonard thought introductions were a complete waste of time. Leonard daydreamed about his last scuba-diving vacation in Belize to ward off the onset of boredom as the rest of the participants filtered into the room.

One minute before the session was scheduled to begin, Kevin ran into the room with his cell phone ringing loudly. He felt a few icy glares from the participants. He answered the call and took the last available seat in the room—next to Leonard. "Julie, thanks for returning my call. I'm going to have to get back to you. I'm attending a Root Cause Analysis workshop that is starting right now. Do not ask me what a Root Cause Analysis workshop is. I have no clue. I'll let you know when I get to the root of it." Kevin laughed smugly at his own joke as he flipped his cell phone closed. He looked over at Leonard, who clearly was not amused by Kevin's humor.

The instructor projected the first slide onto the screen and began to address the group. "Good afternoon, everyone. Are your seat belts fastened? We are going to take a trip down Problem Lane. Keep your eyes on the road. We're looking for signs pointing us in the direction of how and why projects fail. Before we come to the meat of the course, I would like to get to know each of you a little better. I'm going to ask you to interview the person next to you. You'll be responsible for presenting this person to the group. Here is what I want you to find out:

1. What is the person's name?
2. What is his or her role in the organization?
3. What projects is he or she currently working on?
4. How does he or she measure the success of a project?
5. What's a fun fact about this person?

"Go ahead and get started."

Kevin extended his hand to Leonard and said, "Hi, my name is Kevin, do you come here often?"

This time Leonard cracked a smile. He shook Kevin's hand and said, "Not if I can help it. My name is Leonard. I'm a product development manager. Currently, I'm overseeing the rollout of a new software release, and I know a project is successful when it gets done within a month of the original planned delivery date and when it is 80 percent bug-free. How about you, Kevin? What signs do you look for as you roll down 'Problem Lane?'"

Kevin chuckled and said, "Before I launch into a philosophical discourse on safe driving practices on the road of projects, I think you've forgotten to tell me a fun fact about yourself."

"I don't have time for fun, but I wish I were back in Belize, living on a boat and scuba diving all day," Leonard said.

"When did you do that?" asked Kevin.

"Oh, last month," responded Leonard. "Diving has been a passion of mine for over 15 years. My wife knows how irritable I get when I'm away from the water for too long. She and the children dread the winter months. They watch me longingly organize my dive bag. My family has even caught me smelling my neoprene wetsuit. Just the smell of it is enough to bring back memories of diving adventures. Those pitiful forays with my dive equipment, along with my grumpiness, prompted them to give me a gift of a scuba diving vacation in Belize. I'm not sure if it was better for me or for them."

"That's incredible," Kevin said. "I started scuba diving seven years ago when I began working here. I wish I had met you earlier."

Questions for Reflection

Before reading any further, take a few moments to think about the following questions:

1. What makes Leonard willing to share his story about scuba diving?
2. If Kevin had not been a scuba diver, what are some ways he could react to Leonard's story and begin to build rapport?

Analysis

Leonard is begrudgingly attending a mandatory training session. His mind is wandering. He is focused on the work on his desk, dreading the moment he must introduce himself to the group, and daydreaming about scuba diving. Kevin storms into the room at the last minute. Clearly, he is also unexcited about attending the workshop. During his phone conversation, we hear Kevin use humor to make the situation more bearable. Kevin observes that Leonard is more annoyed than amused by his attempt at humor.

After a few opening remarks, the instructor asks the participants to interview one another. Kevin immediately extends a handshake to Leonard and makes another glib comment. This time Leonard manages a smile. As he shakes Kevin's hand, he obligingly rattles off quick answers to the introductory questions listed by the instructor. Leonard matches Kevin's sarcastic tone in his answers. Kevin, realizing that he and Leonard are at least on the surface beginning to connect with one another, takes a risk by humorously nudging Leonard to share a "fun fact."

At first it appears that Leonard will ignore Kevin's nudging by claiming he works too hard to have any fun. However, the drive to connect with Kevin and share his passion for scuba diving overrides Leonard's defense system. In a short story burst, Leonard relives the personal exigencies that brought about his recent trip to Belize. Kevin is amazed. Kevin and Leonard now have more than a shared annoyance at attending a workshop to bind and bond them.

We can all relate to daydreaming during a training event or boring meeting. Leonard's imagination is engaged in his escapist world of scuba diving. Kevin's humor, tone, and general demeanor open a channel of trust between himself and Leonard. Kevin's response of general interest, which in this case is accentuated by his own involvement in scuba diving, creates an opportunity for the two to start sharing more stories and to continue building a bond through them. Once a window of trust is open, the challenge is keeping it open by investing in the relationship in a significant way. If Leonard and Kevin simply swap "war stories" and grand tales of their scuba adventures, their storytelling will result in little more than entertainment, a superficial bond, and mutual ego gratification. If the stories are to act as bonding agents, they must become more and more personal and must probe the other's feelings, attitudes, and perceptions. This is when stories are operating at their fullest potential, and this is what great leaders do when they are focused on the strategic and personal nature of relationships in their organizations.

Vignette #13: Clarence and Amy

Clarence had known for some time that he had to do something about his love life. His work as an independent contractor kept him on the road a lot, so it was next to impossible for him to meet anyone. And because desperate times require desperate measures, Clarence had opened an account with the Dates for Grab telephone dating service. He used to laugh at his friends who dabbled in Internet dating and personal ads.

In an effort to screen unwanted responses, at the beginning of his voice message, Clarence read a poem he had written. He thought his strategy was very clever. Dates for Grab charges callers three dollars a minute to listen to messages. Anyone willing to listen to his poem for three minutes, and who wasn't frightened off before Clarence divulged pieces of personal information ought to at least be interesting on a date, Clarence reasoned.

At any moment, Amy would arrive. He wondered whether they would have anything in common. Clarence stuffed his hands deep into his pockets and braced himself for a long, uncomfortable afternoon.

Amy shuffled up to the bench where Clarence was sitting and nervously asked, "Excuse me, are you Clarence?"

Clarence had been so lost in his own thoughts that he had not noticed the attractive woman approaching him. "Ah, yes I am. You must be Amy."

Amy and Clarence exchanged pleasantries and small talk as they made their way to the Museum of Fine Arts. It was Amy's idea to check out an exhibit of Impressionist paintings. Clarence loved art but hated to analyze it. Whenever he looked at a painting, he tried to feel the mood of the scene as if he were standing in the middle of it.

The exhibition was crowded, and people all around Clarence and Amy were engaged in intense intellectual debates. They began to slowly make their way around the hall. Clarence noticed that Amy was very quiet. She seemed to be absorbed. Clarence felt that he should say something intelligent to impress Amy, but when he opened his mouth he found himself saying something totally unexpected.

"Look at this farm painting. The scene is calm and tranquil but I bet there was a storm the night before." Although Amy's face remained expressionless, Clarence continued. "See the little boy sitting on the fence post? He's sad, but it's not because of the storm. He went to his first dance last night and he was too shy to ask Mary Lou to dance with him. To add insult to injury, he had to stand by as he watched his older brother Marcus dance close with Mary Lou."

Amy's face broke into a slow smile, and she added, "And that boy's mother is going to give him a whipping if he doesn't get the chickens fed before breakfast." Clarence laughed.

Amy batted her eyes flirtatiously and inquired in a teasing but gentle tone, "Have you ever felt like that little boy?"

Amy and Clarence looked into each other's eyes and smiled. This was not going to be a long or uncomfortable afternoon after all.

Questions for Reflection

Before reading any further, take a few moments to think about the following questions:

1. How do Clarence and Amy form a connection with one another? Try to identify the trigger (the specific events, words, and behavior that lead to this connection).
2. How do stories operate on multiple levels in this vignette?

Analysis

Clarence has difficulty meeting women because of his work. Consequently, he establishes a voice mailbox with a telephone dating service. The first instance of storytelling in the vignette occurs before Clarence and Amy have even met.

Clarence takes a novel approach to his message. Facts, he believes, are too dry and uninformative, so he decides to read a poem he has written. The poem is an instance of storytelling. Through the poem, Clarence reveals a piece of his imagination. He goes on to reason that if someone spends the time and money to listen to his poem, is not made uncomfortable by it, and still wants to meet him, then a date with this person should at least be interesting.

When Amy walks up to him, Clarence is too lost in his own worries to even notice her. At Amy's suggestion, they go to the museum.

Clarence is still plagued with worry. Art is an emotional experience for Clarence. He does not like to analyze paintings. Rather, Clarence enjoys immersing himself in a painting's story. He notices that Amy appears to be very absorbed. Clarence wants to impress Amy. Because he knows nothing about her, Clarence decides to say something intellectually stimulating. But when he opens his mouth to comment on a painting, he finds himself telling a story. Initially, as Clarence starts to tell his story, Amy's face remains expressionless, but, as Clarence continues, Amy's face breaks into a smile. She responds by adding a piece to Clarence's story. By doing so, Amy is collaborating with Clarence, and collaboration is an important step toward making them partners.

Amy's addition to Clarence's story causes them to laugh. Once again, we see how humor can break the ice between people and ultimately affirm that a connection between them is being made. Amy moves beyond humor by asking Clarence if he has ever felt like the boy in the painting. Simultaneously, Amy and Clarence look into each others eyes and smile. Clarence affirms that Amy has not been too intrusive with her question. On the contrary, through the use of stories, they have taken a first step toward forming a real bond.

Vignette #14: Helping People Bond

Michael ended his telephone conversation and headed toward the elevators. As CEO and chairman, he had called a press conference for Wall Street financial analysts to go over the company's third-quarter revenue projections. Prospects looked good, and he wanted to get the word out on the street.

Jerry fumbled his way out of the human resources department and stopped for a moment to check his clipboard. His next stop was the executive suite on the 28th floor. He took out his identification badge and pinned it to his shirt; he would need it to gain access to the offices on that floor.

This was Jerry's second week at Allbright Conglomerate, and he hadn't yet gotten into the swing of things. If delivering mail were this difficult, how would he ever climb the corporate ladder and become an executive? he wondered to himself. Jerry stepped into the elevator and absentmindedly thumbed through the packages and envelopes in his cart. He became so engrossed that he didn't notice that the elevator doors had opened on the 28th floor.

Michael got into the elevator and pressed the button for the lobby. Before Jerry realized what had happened, the doors had closed. "Shoot!" Jerry exclaimed. "I needed to get off on the 28th floor."

In his frustration, Jerry dropped the mail he was carrying. Jerry shook his head in disgust. Michael, without a second thought, bent down to pick up the dropped mail and handed it to Jerry. He paused for a moment to look into Jerry's eyes.

"Thanks," Jerry muttered self-consciously. He could feel Michael's concerned gaze searching him. "This is my second week working here, and I'm still trying to learn my delivery route. I am a first-year business studies major at Walton University, but if I keep this up I won't be fit for a job flipping hamburgers."

"I'll never forget my first job," said Michael. "I worked as a receptionist for an automotive company. Have you ever seen one of those old switchboards with plugs and holes?"

"Yeah, you mean like the one featured in that AT&T commercial where the operator is trying to answer a bunch of lines at the same time?" answered Jerry.

"Yes, that was me," Michael mused. "I was the biggest disaster. I could never keep the outgoing lines separated from the incoming lines, and I was constantly hanging up on people. That was the most difficult and chaotic job I have ever had. Certainly taught me to appreciate operators."

The doors of the elevator opened onto the lobby and Michael stepped out. "Good luck, Jerry," Michael said. "My name is Michael. Let me know how you get on."

Questions for Reflection

Before reading any further, take a few moments to think about the following questions:

1. If Michael had not responded to Jerry by telling his switchboard story, what sort of effect would a pep talk or even no response have had on Jerry?
2. What are the specific behaviors Michael exhibits that support the tone and message of his story?

Analysis

Stories act as glue between people. In other words, stories show how our sets of experiences, memories, hopes, fears, and desires match with someone else's. I will be able to understand you, and communicate effectively with you, only when I can relate my stories to your stories.

Stories have the power to bind and bond individuals regardless of their relative position or experience. Michael is a busy CEO with an important press conference to get to, and Jerry is a young man in his first job as a mail clerk for a big corporation.

Jerry is so preoccupied with trying to figure out how to do his job that he does not realize the elevator has reached the 28th floor. Frazzled, Jerry drops a bundle of mail. Michael picks it up and looks into Jerry's eyes. He initially tries to connect with Jerry by making eye contact. Naturally Jerry becomes self-conscious and tries to explain his clumsiness.

His explanation triggers a memory, and Michael decides to share a story about his first job. Notice that Michael begins his story in the form of a question, which is a way to involve Jerry. When Jerry answers, he must transcend his own predicament and vicariously imagine Michael's first job experience as a switchboard operator.

Why doesn't Michael just give Jerry a pep talk? He could have easily said something like, "Well, son, I remember my first job and it wasn't easy. You need to keep your nose to the grindstone and believe in yourself. With hard work and a little luck, who knows? Maybe you'll be CEO of a company one day."

Michael does not give a pep talk because he knows how ineffective it would be. He does not want to distance himself from Jerry; he wants to connect with him. Michael completes the bond by noticing Jerry's name badge. He wishes Jerry good luck and invites him to seek another opportunity to continue their discussion.

Time and again I have witnessed the magic of people forming bonds with one another during training workshops. In one striking example, I was facilitating a workshop for a company that was going through massive layoffs. Employees were fairly certain that their plant was going to be shut down and that many of them would either be laid off or relocated. Morale was not good, and people were less than enthusiastic to be attending a communications workshop.

I began the workshop with a series of exercises aimed at getting participants to bind and bond with one another. I did not expect miracles, but the results amazed us all. One quiet, conservatively dressed woman with two children related her adventures as a Harley-Davidson biker and brought in pictures to show the class. Another woman shared her passion for home craft projects and brought in a number of examples. Someone else revealed his hobby as an emergency ham radio operator. By the end of the workshop, people had discovered a wealth of stories and experiences. These stories enabled them to see past their real and legitimate fears about the future.

STORIES AS WEAPONS

Like anything else, stories are neutral. *How* we use them determines their impact. Stories can be used in destructive and aggressive ways. For example, they can be purposely misleading. In some contexts, the word "story" implies that the speaker is lying. Perhaps someone is telling a tall tale or simply misconstruing facts to influence the listener in a negative way. Either way, stories are being consciously used as weapons.

Stories can be very convincing. Think about how stories were used to fuel the Cold War. The Communists ran a propaganda machine. Exaggerations and outright lies were constructed to glorify Communism and portray the United States as a villain. Likewise, the United States was just as guilty of using stories to promote fear of Communism. Stories can be used to manipulate people's thoughts and feelings.

Character attacks in political campaigns are another example of how stories can be used to manipulate. Although character attacks are perceived as negative, campaign strategists resort to them because they are so effective. These attacks involve telling stories that cast the opposing candidate in a negative light. Once a story is told, it is likely to stick in people's minds. After the fact, candidates apologize and retreat from character assassinations, but it doesn't really matter because the stories have already had their effect.

In a legal and business settings, stories are used to support arguments and make convincing cases. The presentation and interpretation of statistical data is a form of storytelling and frequently is used to support a particular agenda. On Wall Street the analysis of a company's financials and performance indicators has been known to dramatically affect the valuation of a company. Most of the time, these valuations are fair, but occasionally people have used data to tell a story that misrepresents a company.

The stronger someone internally believes his or her own stories, the more convincing the stories can be. The stories we tell ourselves create our realities. We've all been victims of believing a story that turns out to be a tool for furthering someone else's agenda. Taken to an extreme, this is what con artists do. They are capable of painting such a powerful picture that we become easily swayed. Con artists and pathological liars frequently succeed in manipulating because their stories are so convincing and believable.

Stories are powerful and can be used for self-serving goals. Gut instinct is the best defense and warning system against stories used as weapons. It can be hard to detect manipulative stories, but if you pay attention to cues—such as the context in which the story is used and the possible motivations someone may have for telling a story—and note other stories that conflict with the one you are being told, then you stand a better chance of avoiding deception. If we can help it, we do not want to be deceived by a false story; therefore, sometimes (as in the story of *The Emperor's New Clothes*) we may have to stand up against common opinion to dispel a myth.

Leaders must be very careful about using stories as weapons. Every effort should be made to use other tactics before employing stories to attack others or spread misinformation. Once you use a story as a weapon, it is very unlikely that you will regain the trust of the recipient of your attack. For anyone, especially leaders, burning bridges of trust and credibility is catastrophic for relationships.

STORIES FOR HEALING

On the other hand, stories also play a central role in relationships by promoting healing. Relationships are damaged by the natural rhythms of people coexisting. Without proper healing, this damage can be long-lasting and can be difficult and even impossible to heal. Stories open channels of communication and allow meaningful conversation about the experiences and perceptions that hinder trust and positive energy.

Stories stimulate our imagination. Significant healing can occur through stories. For example, many schools of therapy incorporate narratives or storytelling as a key part of the healing process. Individuals work through their past or current issues by speaking about their experiences. Healing occurs when individuals realize they are not locked into behaviors, thoughts, feelings, self-perceptions, or beliefs reflected in their stories. By working through their stories and gaining insights, they can begin to envision new possibilities.

The right story told at the right time can help another person, and this is the principal way leaders can promote healing in their organizations. In this regard, everyone in the organization needs to be a leader. Recall the story of Michael the CEO and Jerry the mail clerk. Recognizing that Jerry was struggling with his job, Michael shared his experience of how badly he bungled his first job as a telephone operator. Michael's story allows Jerry to rewrite his own. Left to his own perceptions, Jerry is likely to believe he is incapable of climbing the corporate ladder if he cannot even deliver mail. Michael's story is liberating and healing.

Sharing stories also promotes healing when there is tension or conflict in an organization. Strained relationships require the attention of a leader who can introduce healing. The fact that stories involve active listening means that listeners can gain a perspective different from their own. By doing so, misunderstandings and breakdowns in communications can be overcome. Healing becomes possible with a willingness to embrace other perspectives. Stories are the most efficient way of communicating these perspectives and catalyzing healing.

I like to simplify leadership by defining it in terms of two key characteristics inherent in meaningful relationships: awareness of self and awareness of others. Becoming aware of who and how we are relieves the tremendous burden of our need to prove or justify ourselves to others. A failure to acknowledge strengths and weaknesses can create unnecessary friction between people. When we feel like we are not understood, appreciated, or when we feel compelled to prove ourselves to others, breakdowns in communication occur and relationships suffer. Our worldview and ingrained reactions to people and events sits below our conscious awareness. Stories are a great tool for reflecting on our experiences. We use these experiences to scrutinize patterns of behavior. Our experiences captured in stories provide clues about our makeup and highlight some of the factors that have influenced our development. A similar line of reasoning applies to the role of stories and awareness of others. Here's the good news: regardless of one's personality, thinking style, communication style, or any other facet of uniqueness, everyone can benefit from working with stories. They are an essential vehicle for developing better awareness of ourselves and awareness of others.

Stories help leaders heal themselves by promoting reflection and greater self-awareness. Likewise, stories enable leaders to promote healing in others. Leaders encounter many broken relationships in organizations that they must attempt to heal. It doesn't matter whether they were a contributor to the damaged relationship. Leaders must play a healing role regardless of how or when people become estranged. Eliciting people's painful and hurtful experiences shared in stories produces a climate for healing. A leader may also need to risk being vulnerable with members of the organization by telling a personal story. Sharing our personal experiences in an honest, earnest fashion may stimulate insight and healing in others. Think about 12-step programs in which members offer support to one another as they share their personal stories. One person's story becomes another person's path to new insights and healing.

Stories heal because they help us vividly remember and relive our experiences. They help us put the fragments of our lives together and reassemble them in ways that recreate the events of our life. Through stories we can find wholeness. Thomas Moore, in his book *Dark Nights of the Soul: A Guide to Finding Your Way Through Life's Ordeals,* puts it this way:

> The repeated telling of a story gradually allows the pieces of life experience to find their relation to each other. Not only the listener, but the teller of a story, too, experiences a catharsis in the telling. If you can find good words and style for your story, you may feel cleansed by it. A story of what you are going through gives your experience form, places it outside yourself and others, and gives the aesthetic pleasure that a good story offers. Whether it is an artful story or a simple report on a life experience, a good story requires a certain clarity that comes from honesty and the willingness to forego excuses, caveats, and explanations. (p. 58)

Where stories and healing are concerned, leaders have two responsibilities. First they must exhibit circumspection. Divulging intimate details is neither necessary nor, in most instances, productive. However, leaders must model reflective behaviors in relation to their experiences within the organization and how those experiences have affected them as a person. Second, leaders must cultivate trust and strong relationships with people in the organization. A leader's power is given by the people who give her or him permission to help them discover insights and embrace healing.

The Story of Victor

Below is a very personal account of a dear colleague. Hal Kane's son Victor died, and, as part of the grieving process, I encouraged Hal to reflect on his son's life in the form of a short narrative. At first Hal was reluctant. The pain of Victor's death was too near. He was also concerned about disrespecting or trivializing his son's death by writing a narrative. After some thought, he put aside his reservations and wrote. The results took us both by surprise. Weaving together a narrative came out in three intense bursts of writing, which Hal described as profoundly cathartic. Hal's story process was deeply healing for him, and it is a testament to the power of story. Through the emergence and natural arrangement of the stories, Hal experienced heartfelt insights and depth of meaning from the void of pain that was previously unavailable to him. Later in the book, a technique called story collaging for piecing together multiple stories is explored.

Ursula and I had just gotten married the day before, and now my new stepson, Victor, who had a paper route obligation to meet, needed a ride to the station where his papers were stored. I woke up at 4:30 A.M. to a fresh carpet of snow, a blowing snowstorm, and a car window that resembled ground glass. Victor shivered in his coat, waiting for the heater to thaw the inside of the car while I scraped at the window with a kitchen spatula, creating a space that would pass for a porthole if we were a ship.

I shifted into first gear and crept out into what I hoped was the street and not the neighbor's front lawn. I kept the car in first gear all the way to the station, wondering if Victor was really going to go through with his commitment. He emerged from his cocoon and began whistling a popular tune as though snow, cold wind, and early winter mornings were not obstacles to happiness, but background scenery to the excitement he felt of having a job, making pocket money, and feeling part of a long tradition of road warriors who delivered newspapers with postal dedication. He was fearless, a trait that would serve him well throughout his life, and I was proud to be part of his family.

Living with Victor through his young adulthood increased my admiration at his ability to put discomfort on the shelf when it came to helping others with their problems, or simply enjoying a heavy class schedule, music lessons, and competitive sports. He was smart, and his lessons came easy. He was agile, and his ability to run for miles at the beach left me in the role of spectator and cheerleader. When he decided to live with his father at the age of 16, I knew that I wouldn't see him again until he entered college and that I would miss his transition to young adulthood. On the other hand, he needed to find out who his father and new stepmother were and whether his other family had the meaning he was after. Our close connection ended that day, although it would take years to find out what the move really meant to all of us.

It didn't work the way he probably wanted it to, but he survived and entered college with his usual enthusiasm for adventure and learning. In the summer, he returned to our house in order to put in long, lucrative hours at Chevrolet to earn his tuition, raiding our refrigerator in the early hours of the morning to satisfy his voracious appetite, and leaving us notes of thanks scattered throughout the house. We were happy to have him back, even temporarily.

Victor had studied over the years to take the California bar exam, first as a part-time student at an unaccredited law school where the political climate matched his own fervor for organizing a bus driver's union in Los Angeles and later as a full-time member of an accredited academy where he learned the rules of evidence and how to handle himself in a courtroom without being threatened with contempt. (You see, Victor was passionate when it came to righting wrongs, and his passion often spilled over the edge of decorum, upsetting the man on the bench who wanted to keep due process under control.) He had taken the bar exam twice and failed both times, giving as reasons that he had his own interpretation of the law that far exceeded what the examiners wanted for an answer. When the day came to take the bar exam for the third time, Victor showed up at the auditorium, took his seat, and settled in for the long hours of anxiety and tedium that we generally feel when something important is on the line. I didn't hear from him after that and began to wonder if he failed the test again and was embarrassed to tell me.

Two weeks later, I was working in the house when the front doorbell chimed. I looked out and saw Victor standing on the front step, faintly whistling a tune and combing his blond hair away from his forehead with his fingers. I opened the door, and, at the same moment, he opened his mouth in a big grin and said, "I passed the bar. I knew I had it made from the first question." After showering him with congratulations I asked why the first question gave him the confidence to finish the test in a way that convinced the examiners he knew what he was talking about, mentally crossing my fingers that it was all true.

"Simple," he replied, "I had studied that particular question on property rights the night before and came back with a crisp, clear description of how to settle the case. My guess is they didn't need to read that critically once I demonstrated that I knew my stuff." I barely contained my excitement and asked him to come in, but he was making the rounds of friends and family and couldn't stay. He did accept my invitation to dinner for the following Saturday. As he drove off, I called his mother and relayed the good news.

That night we toasted his triumph and began thinking about his future as a bona fide lawyer, licensed finally to charge all windmills in the city by the sea.

Like any normal male his age, Victor decided it was time to settle down and get married. He was practicing immigration law in Los Angeles, working with two Vietnamese paralegals to build and service his caseload. One of Victor's assistants suggested he travel to Vietnam to meet a distant relative who would introduce him to an eligible woman. Victor asked for the woman's address and began writing her letters. She eagerly replied in a carefully scribed mixture of English, French, and Vietnamese. Her letters were hesitant at first, asking for his "bona fides" in the way that strangers look warily across the room at an attractive suitor who has made eye contact. Victor, with his fine command of the English language, responded in ways that ignited her ardor, and the letters of inquiry soon gave way to letters of passion.

Victor flew to Vietnam and met his "pen pal" and her family. He fell in love with her during his two-week stay as they enjoyed each other's company at the beach, in romps through the city on a motorbike, and at family dinners where sign language and smiles passed for pleasant conversation. He returned to his work and began devoting a good chunk of his time to filling out immigration papers so that she could come to this country within the year (the normal wait being two years or longer) and they could start their married life. In the meantime, his wife-to-be began planning a traditional Vietnamese wedding to be held in Vietnam in the near future. They continued their letter writing campaign, exchanging vows of eternal love across an ocean of time and space.

Victor returned to Vietnam for the wedding a few months later, and the videos taken at the events surrounding the wedding show a smiling, if somewhat dazed, Victor being stage-managed by his friends and bride through the various ceremonies that surround a traditional wedding, including family gatherings, a song fest at a night club, and introductions to the family hierarchy. It was over all too soon, and Victor soon found himself flying home, alone once again.

Over the next few months, her letters took on a different tone. She began complaining about the length of time it took to manage the immigration process on his end. Then lightening struck. One day a letter arrived from her and he eagerly opened it. It was not good news. She had decided, she wrote, that she didn't want to continue the marriage, that she had found an old boyfriend who owned a restaurant in Vietnam and she wanted a divorce to marry him. Victor was shocked to the core. Nothing, absolutely nothing, had prepared him for this declaration. He immediately flew back to Vietnam and confronted her with his concerns.

She declared flatly that the marriage had been a mistake from the beginning and that there was no chance of stopping the divorce proceedings in her country. Furthermore, she did not want to continue their exchange of letters or have him call at anytime. It was over, period. Victor flew home, exhausted and confused, unable to fathom what had happened or why it had happened. A naturally upbeat person, he suffered his loss in silence and we could only imagine the hell he was going through. It was shortly after this incident that the first signs of his fatal illness appeared.

Victor's courage never wavered as he began the series of psychological and physical tests that would reveal the nature of his illness. His friends had noticed instances of odd behavior in the past, attributing vacant stares and lapses of memory as reflections of someone who was heavily burdened with the immigration problems of his clients, his union organizing, and a gradual recovery from his traumatic divorce. Suddenly, he decided to leave his practice and Los Angeles, a move his friends thought was related to his need for a change of scenery and a fresh start. It was only later, when the test results were in, that his mother and I saw that it was an instinctive move to be closer to his family in time of need. At a deeper level, we were convinced now that he was frightened by the mental changes beginning to take place, and we knew that we would support him in whatever healing he needed to go through.

He found an apartment in San Francisco and lived there for a few months. His mental abilities continued to decline. He moved again, into a small room off an apartment filled with other adults and children, hoping to reduce his feeling of alienation by surrounding himself with others. But things continued to slide downhill. Finally, his mother and sister found a way to get him into the major HMO in northern California and, once he had membership, found a doctor who referred him for neuropsychological testing. The test results were shattering.

On certain scales, this bright, attentive, socially conscious person had the IQ of the severely retarded. The signs and symptoms he displayed, added to the results of seven hours' worth of testing, revealed a man who was suffering from frontal-temporal dementia, an insidious and fatal neurodegenerative disease, a kind of reverse Alzheimer's that destroys the so-called executive functions of the cortex (planning, judgment, reasoning, etc.) in the front of the brain and gradually works itself toward the rear, obliterating sense and memory.

Victor, his mother, and I met with the head psychiatrist to review the test results and discuss treatment options. I vividly remember the psychiatrist calmly telling Victor that he had dementia and that no treatment as yet existed for his condition. He delivered his message by staring at his shoes until Victor's mother practically shouted, "Look at him. Tell it to him." The doctor snapped his head up, as though he just remembered his duty as a healer, and continued his monologue. Victor shook his head vehemently and declared that he didn't have dementia and didn't believe the tests or the doctor. We left the office with heavy hearts and a determination to do our best to see that Victor's last days were comfortable. From that point on, the psychiatrist became known in our family as Dr. Shoes.

The next months were filled with research into assisted living facilities, nursing homes, social security disability claims, support groups, Web sites on the nature of the illness, and preparations for moving Victor into our house. Victor moved in (he needed no encouragement) in December 1990, and we could see the changes taking place in his ability to focus on something as simple as watching a movie, driving his truck, or articulating his needs. As the illness progressed, his language became simpler, and, at times, he became mute. He soon developed tremors in his throat, neck, and chest (called fasciculations), a sign that something else was wrong. We arranged for him to have a complete neurological workup at the University of California, San Francisco (UCSF), and discovered that, in addition to his dementia, he had now developed Lou Gehrig's disease (amyotrophic lateral sclerosis, or ALS), a fatal malady that would shorten his life to less than two years. I called it nature's double-whammy, as if one death sentence wasn't enough.

When Victor became too difficult for us to handle (eloping out the front door and ambling down the street in search of pennies), we made arrangements with a nearby assisted care facility to provide his room and board. We met with Cynthia, the director, and toured the home, meeting the staff and getting a feel for the place. It was a warm, accepting environment with real caregivers, and we agreed to bring him in the next week. The transfer was uneventful, because by this time Victor had little cognition left and was, for all intents and purposes, mute.

His room resembled a college dorm, complete with a refrigerator for his favorite drinks and fruit bars, a new color TV and easy chair, a large desk, a comfortable single bed, a private washroom, a cabinet for his clothes, and room to work on his art. We went home that afternoon breathing deep sighs of relief that he was in good hands and that we could begin to retrieve our lives from the intensity of the caregiving we had been doing for the past two years. We visited Victor often and took him to outdoor concerts, supermarkets, and walks in the park until near his end, when walking became an effort. His sister drove up from San Francisco every Sunday to engage him in similar activities, leaving her family at home to make her brother's last days meaningful and joyous.

In the last months of his life, Victor stopped eating with the exception of ice cream and lemonade. He grew thin and gaunt, and at times doubled over while walking as his back muscles and nerves succumbed to the ravages of ALS. We had enrolled the services of the hospice program at Kaiser Permanente, and they had started visiting him on a weekly basis to ensure his comfort and educate the staff on what to expect in his final days.

We got the final call on a Friday morning, April 23, 2004. He had fallen in the shower and wasn't moving. My wife said that she would run over and let me know if I was needed (it was early and I was still in my pajamas), and she dashed out the door. The phone rang 20 minutes later with the news that he had died peacefully, the apparent victim of a heart that gave out as he was doing his morning routine. (Nature was merciful; he could have asphyxiated and drowned in his own juices.)

We had promised his body to science, and an ambulance arrived soon after to take the body to autopsy at UCSF. We went home to make the requisite calls, realizing that it was over for him but not for us.

It is now some eight months later and his memory echoes throughout the house. It's our first Christmas without him, and it will be difficult. A picture of him adorns our living room. He's riding on the back of a motor scooter in Saigon, a pleasant grin plastered across his wind-whipped face as he speeds off to celebrate his marriage. He has no idea of what the future holds, and that's as it should be since life isn't lived in the future (or the past) but in the moment. I've known him for over 40 years, helped raise him to manhood, consoled him when times were tough, and cheered him on when success came knocking at his door. He's gone to wherever fighters of the good fight go. I'd like to catch up with him someday and trade some wonderful stories.

Commentary on Victor's Story

I was compelled to share this deeply moving account because of its personal nature. It's a dramatic example of the ability of stories to promote healing. Beyond the piece's emotional qualities, it demonstrates the essential overriding thrust to this book—stories allow us to communicate in profoundly deep and meaningful ways with ourselves and others. The purpose of including Hal's stories was to glimpse the interior life of stories. Capturing a reflective stream of stories is something all of us, whether we are leaders or not, need to be engaged in.

Hal's stories together create a collage of memories. These stories hint at the cathartic benefits they provide to Hal and his family. Connected to these stories are many others that surface as Hal and his family relive the ones he has shared. These stories are portals to a wealth of other experiences and insights. Recollecting these stories provides meaning and context. The vexing and irreconcilable existential questions surrounding the nature of death finds a home in the stories. In our stories we can find a peace that comes from the stillness offered by an engaged imagination and active heart. Our analytical minds cannot fully fathom heavy issues such as why a young man dies, but our imaginations and hearts can explore the nooks and crannies of our stories to find poignant solace. Reasons become less important than depth; and interwoven stories contain a wealth of depth.

If you are interested in reading other examples of how stories promote healing in a therapeutic way, I recommend Erica Helm Meade's book, *Tell It By Heart: Women and the Healing Power of Story.* Now that we have seen an example of stories healing on a very personal level, let's turn our attention to how stories help leaders promote healing in an organizational setting.

Vignette #15: Market Peril

Dan stepped out of the sanctity of his plush office. Being senior vice president of marketing and communications for a major Fortune 500 company had its perks but was not without a lot of challenges. Sales figures for the quarter were way down and people were nervous. Reorganizations were likely—that seemed to always be the executive team's answer to complex problems. The company's major new product launch was flopping. Everyone had had grand—and, as far as Dan was concerned, unrealistic—expectations that the new product would revitalize the company's shrinking market share. At the moment, there was a lot of confusion and finger-pointing going on, and much of it was being directed toward the marketing and communications department. Dan sighed to himself. He owed his team some answers, but he wasn't sure what he was going to tell them.

Twenty of Dan's senior-level directors and managers were waiting for him in a conference room. The room was silent, and, except for some nervous fidgeting, people were stiff and on edge. Dan realized that many of the rumors flying around the company had created significant rifts within his team. No one wanted to take the blame, and people were not talking as blame was passed around to different people without reason. Dan had always prided himself on the cohesive camaraderie displayed by his team. He had a lot of respect for his team's talents. However, even strong teams can break down easily when the pressure is high and trust and communication are low. If the marketing and communications team was going to have any chance of figuring what it could do differently to help the product succeed, Dan had to help people mend some relationships.

Dan's assistant had prepared an elaborate presentation crammed with data and strategic recommendations. The projector in the room was already switched on; all Dan needed to do was plug in his laptop. At the last moment, Dan switched off the projector and walked from the front of the room to take a vacant chair in the middle of the conference table.

"Good morning," said Dan. "Under the circumstances, I am opting to skip the presentation. I'll e-mail all of you a copy, but I think our time this morning will be better spent talking about your candid views of our current state of affairs. I must confess I am no less confused than any of you. I won't lie to you; the company's executive team feels the new products' abysmal performance is attributable to our failure to adequately define market segments, develop the product's branding, and create compelling collaterals." Dan paused to scan the faces around the room. People's faces were flushed. Darting glares were being thrown around the table.

Dan continued, "As I was grilled by the executive team, I had a flashback to one of my early experiences in a consulting firm. I was a junior member of a large team working deep in the trenches, assigned the laborious work of data analysis. Early in the project it became clear to many of us that the clients' real issues were not being addressed. Almost everyone on the consulting team started to become wary and suspicious of the lead consultant's motives. We were waiting for the bomb to drop at any minute. Rumor had it that the lead consultant was doing a favor for one of his business school buddies who needed to justify the strategy he had put in place in order to save his job. The whole team of consultants was walking on eggshells. We spent less and less time communicating with each other, and collaboration went completely out the window. To borrow a cliché, the emperor had no clothes, and no was going to speak up. I watched my relationships with my peers that had otherwise been strong erode in front of my eyes. We were all part of a sham waiting for the axe to fall. It made me realize how fragile my working relationships were. Some of the relationships never fully recovered from the fallout of the project. We all got blamed for the hiring company's eventual dissatisfaction with our recommendations. Ironically, those of us sitting on the lower end of the consulting team pecking order took the brunt of the blame. Granted, it was beyond my control to change the nature of the consulting intervention, but in retrospect I should have never let my relationships fall apart. If the team of consultants had maintained more open lines of communication we may have even found a way to make lemonade out of a lemon."

"There is no doubt in my mind; we are going through something very similar right now in our own company. I am not on a crusade to pin blame on anyone today, and if anyone should step up to the plate to take the heat it will be me. I certainly do not agree with most of the criticisms of the marketing and communications department that are flying around the company; however, I'm sure we can come up with some ideas to improve the situation. First I want to give you guys a chance to tell your stories. None of us have been privy to all of the intricate and interdependent details surrounding the company's product launch. So let's take 30 minutes and break into groups of four to share our impressions with each other. Then we can reconvene the entire group to report and look for some common ground. Don't hold back in your groups. Lay it all out—the good, the bad, the ugly, and your thoughts on what we can do differently going forward."

Questions for Reflection

Before reading any further, take a few moments to think about the following questions:

1. What are some specific things Dan does and says to promote healing with the group?
2. How does Dan use his personal story to promote healing?
3. Is Dan's story enough to heal the group and help mend its relationships?

Analysis

From the beginning of the vignette Dan exhibits the signs of a good leader. He is reflective, aware of himself, and aware of others. Dan realizes his first course of action is to mend the strained relationships in his team. His decision to forego the presentation and sit down with the group creates an environment of vulnerability. Dan must gain the trust of the group. In quick order, Dan acknowledges and validates the emotions of the group. Then he tells his team a story. The story is rich with other story references, thus increasing its communication effectiveness. The main thrust of Dan's story is not to deliver a specific message. He uses the story to invite people to open up with one another. Dan models the behavior he wants his team to adopt. A group of 20 is too large for the kind of healing conversations that are required, so Dan breaks them into smaller groups and instructs them to share their experiences by being as specific as possible. Believe it or not, you don't need to do much to get people to tell their stories because we do it naturally under the right conditions. This is not foolproof. You will never get 100 percent participation—but then you never do, regardless of the strategy. Having people converse in small groups will yield amazing results. People open their floodgates and gush with thoughts. From all the sharing, new connections and ties are developed and people become invigorated with new ideas, hopes, and possibilities. In short, they have new stories to tell and live.

SUMMARY

Strong leaders focus on relationships. With the aid of stories, leaders can become more aware of themselves and others. Leaders put stories to work in their relationships by using them to build and maintain strong bonds and promote healing through active listening. Stories can also be used as weapons with potentially negative effects.

6 / Case Study—Environment for Organizational Improvement (E.O.I.)

I MET BRUCE Rector and was immediately struck by his story. With a twinkle in his eye and a smile ever-ready, Bruce found his voice as a leader through a series of rich experiences, and, as he would say, "some good luck." Our paths crossed accidentally and we quickly formed a bond around our shared passion for helping organizations develop their heart and soul while fattening their bottom lines. After his success in the wine industry, Bruce took a deep breath and a stepped back to reflect on his stories and figure out where to go next.

Bruce has taken his stories and transformed them into a physical estate known as the Environment for Organizational Improvement (E.O.I.). This is a magical place where groups in various stages of organizational development can come to gain perspective. In the narrative, observe how Bruce's relationship to wine, the art of blending, the business of production, and the people he worked with enabled him to imagine the nature of leadership. Bruce's stories are the cornerstone of realizing his dream and helping others to find theirs.

Developing leaders through the power of narrative and the metaphor of wine is the mission of E.O.I. Bruce credits his development as a leader of one of the most successful California wineries to the power of stories. Bruce puts it this way, "People and wine improve in a similar fashion. With the proper care and blending, they mature into high-performing assets. The Environment for Organizational Improvement offers a hands-on approach to growth and development." In this chapter, Bruce shares his story. As you read, pay careful attention to his explanation of the difference between mixing and blending. Bruce's passion for developing leaders who are capable of blending the talents of people to create high-performing teams is at the heart of E.O.I.'s work. The effectiveness of E.O.I.'s approach rests in a methodology of teaching leaders how to build strong relationships in their organizations through stories' abilities to help people bond with one another and promote healing.

The Story of E.O.I.

In 1979 I drove up to my new place of winemaking employment. It was the beautiful old Ruby Hill Winery in the Livermore Valley, which was called Stony Ridge at the time. As I parked my VW bus, I saw that standing five feet in front of me was a woman. Even though I was looking at her back, I could tell that I had never seen her before. She was about to throw a pair of pliers to a man who was up on the roof. She was middle-aged, though she had a girlish way about her. When she threw the pliers, she didn't let go of them at the right moment to get them up on the roof. Instead, she held onto them just a microsecond too long and they came straight back and crumpled the windshield.. Everybody had a good laugh. That husband and wife turned out to be Helen and Bruno Benziger, my new employers.

Within two years, we were all on a rocket ride together. The Benziger family, Mark Stornetta, and myself became involved with a new winery called Glen Ellen Winery. We built the production from zero to 4 million cases in 12 years, all during a declining market for the overall wine industry. During the course of these 12 years, I had my "15 minutes of fame." For two or three years, I sourced, blended, and bottled more Chardonnay into 750-milliliter bottles than anyone else in the world. In 1993, we sold the winery at what turned out to be its pinnacle. That case volume was never exceeded. Our successes and the special story culture of Glen Ellen Winery were not carried forward.

Let me tell you a little more about how we grew a successful business on the leadership principles of stories. The eldest Benziger son, Mike, had a dream to create a boutique winery. With the help of my brother-in-law Tom, he found a stunning piece of property in Glen Ellen, California, just below Jack London State Park. Mike made a down-payment on an old farmhouse on 80 acres with the help of Helen Benziger's mother's money. Then, the rest of the Benziger family migrated west from New York. It was one big happy and very exciting family, and I was part of it as the consulting winemaker at the time.

As things unfolded, it became increasingly obvious that Bruno Benziger, the patriarch, didn't understand that wine had to age. His mindset was different than ours. It was different because he had been the first person to figure out how to import Scotch whiskey in a boat, in bulk, and bottle it on this continent. Because of this, he had a one-dollar advantage on the retail shelf compared to other bottles of Scotch. Bruno, his brother, and partners were able to build a million-case brand of Scotch whiskey under the trademark of Harvey's. So Bruno's standard of production-timing with the whiskey was to get the goods cleared, bottle them, and let the Scotch hit the market all within a week.

To defend our dream, Mike and I had to do something to get Bruno off our backs. We needed to give our dream product time to mature, so we created a cash-flow wine called Glen Ellen Proprietor's Reserve. Now Bruno could go out and sell something. He could chum it up with his old family friends and Marine Corps buddies who were his broker network, while leaving Mike and I alone to create our own boutique wine. The first wines that we made for Bruno were a red and a white. The red was Cabernet Sauvignon, and the white was made from two grapes: 50 percent French Columbard for its acidity, and 50 percent Chardonnay for its lushness.

Then the fateful moment happened. Bruno was back in New York with his buddies, kicking around ideas on how to "create the condition" to sell more wine. He got on the telephone and called back to the winery. I was the one that picked up the phone. He asked me if we could put another 25 percent of Chardonnay into the wine so we could label it Chardonnay instead of just white wine. I said, "Ah, sure." I remember hanging up the phone and turning to Mike, and saying to him, "Well, here we go."

Where we went was on a blending odyssey. That's how we kept the supply up with the demand. We did it by blending. Blending also became a powerful metaphor for us. Now blending is different than mixing. In mixing, one of the components is better than the finished compilation. In blending, the finished blend is better than any single component. Synergy in action. When one blends, there needs to be an experienced practitioner and a careful palate that knows how to bring up the rear, and not dull the leaders. The winemaker must understand what precise components will come together to create the perfectly blended product. This requires several considerations.

So, when I start to blend, this is what I consider: I draw my attention to the wines with the oddest qualities and the ones with the more banal qualities. These are the individual lots in the wine inventory that need the most help. These are also the exact same types of individuals in a business organization that need the most help. The wine components, as well as the individuals of an organization, if left without help, can poison any effort to excel. And don't think you can just fire these jokers and jerks or sell them in bulk like wine. Relatively speaking, they will always be with you. Every organization has two extremes. So the heart has to soften to understand how they need help. You don't do it by sacrificing your best (that's mixing), you do it by synergizing your best (that's blending). And with that right touch, with that right blending, another dream of improvement within an organization can start to happen.

So that's what we did, both on the wine front and on the leadership front. It all happened because I and others were allowed to do what we do best, which is to use our skills to blend our hearts away.

As a matter of fact, after a couple of years of producing Proprietor's Reserve, our dream of a boutique winery, which we had kept alive, was eclipsed. But as with all eclipses, the light emerges later. At the time, our winery with a 20,000-case use-permit was now bottling around the clock and producing 1 million cases around the clock. I asked Bruno, "How big are we going to let this thing get?"

The answer? Well you have to understand something about Bruno. He was a great leader because he was a great storyteller. Bruno had a gift for using stories to build strong relationships. His stories created trust and he encouraged us to share our own stories, all of which became a thriving part of our winery's social fabric. Because of the trust he inspired and the dynamic interpersonal environment he cultivated, Bruno could tell a story in a single sentence and it would become our steadfast principles of operation. So Bruno answered my question of how big were we going to let the winery get with one of his classic short stories.

He said, "Bruce, as big as the marketplace wants us to get, because, remember, when you are touched with it … run as hard and as fast as you can, because you may never be touched with it again." So that's the story I accepted, and that's what we did. And of course, the plot did thicken.

Before Bruno passed away peacefully in his sleep in 1989, he brought in a master organizational development consultant and storyteller by the name of Jim Clark. This guy had a way of eliciting our visions and dreams in the form of stories and getting us to believe them. Jim set the stage for a bunch of 30-somethings to carry on as general partners of the winery after Bruno passed away. We were able to sell more wine than we had ever sold before. We increased our sales volume to more than 2 million cases.

We did this by employing some master storytellers. Jim made us see that we had very good principles and standards in place, and we, as the general partners, should stop doing so many tasks that could be done by others and start managing the will and hope of the organization.

Just to make sure we understood what he was saying, Jim broke the code for us. During one meeting he said to us, "You know, if you stop hiring from without, and start hiring from within, you'll be amazed at what happens." He taught us how to give employees the keys to the highway of hope. That's how he wanted us to lead. Jim wanted us to create conditions in the winery in which a person wouldn't have someone brought in from the outside to be their boss. Instead, that person would grow into becoming a "boss."

I put the word "boss" in quotation marks because we considered bosses to be not just people who exert their will on others, but rather the people who train their replacement as the company expands. The concept of boss-as-thug was gone, and the reality of boss-as-coach-trainer-organizer had arrived. Jim had planted a seed in our imaginations that became a critical operating story for us.

For me, this operating story of leadership was the genesis of what later became my vision of E.O.I. We took Jim's story and let it grow for all of our employees. It led to the creation of the winery's "Ed Center," which was an educational center with a diverse curriculum and teaching staff, many of whom were our employees. This enabled our employees to do what we were doing as owners—that is, it allowed them to be trainers and to tell their own stories. These were dollars well spent, because they yielded rich returns from our employees and customers alike. As partners we were hooked on organizational development work. This new approach of blending skills glued the company together in the absence of our patriarch.

This overall experience convinced me that, in the context of the workplace, a lot more can be done for human development than what was being done at the time. However, this timing converged with becoming a member of what I called the 40-40 Club. This name was coined by an observation that I had: when enough of your partners turn 40 years old and you owe the bank $40 million, you start to look at things differently. And that's what we did.

A doable scenario that could address our competitive situation was vertical integration on our part and loan syndication on the bank's part. But we decided to not follow through with that scenario because we were now in a maturing segment and we knew the margins would go lower and lower. Besides, the timing was right to live out our original dreams. So in late 1993 we sold the winery, and the Benziger family carried on in a wonderful way.

I was the one who took the "road less traveled." This path was more challenging than anticipated and included a shedding of the power side of my professional identity. I was a changed person. I used to be the guy who people viewed as being at the top of the organization on the production side, the person who was helping 250 grower families make enough money to buy a new car or put their kids through college. I got a clue of the change when I was stood up for lunch for the first time. I was now an option on people's social calendars rather than an imperative. That was okay; it was even good for me. It gave me the opportunity to drop an identity and start a new dream.

The dream is forming around what Jim Clark encouraged us to dream about: inspire the will, spirit, and hope of everyone around you so that they are transformed into leaders. Here enters my vision for building E.O.I. I'm not sure if I can do this directly, but I am very certain that if there is an enriched environment for people to work in while they are doing this transformative work themselves, I can increase the chances of it happening and sticking.

Probably the best way that I can do this is to share what a decade of dynamic contemplation produced. My last decade of work produced an informal garden, buildings, and a reflective environment that inspires and encourages storytelling. The environment that was created was created because I was and am in the process of working out my own ideas and energy outdoors. I have developed a dream to blend my amateur doings with my professional skill. It is called the **E**nvironment for **O**rganizational **I**mprovement, or E.O.I. This dream weaves together avocation and profession and takes up where our powerhouse of organizational development had come to an end in its previous form with Glen Ellen Winery.

E.O.I. is creating a way of developing tomorrow's leaders through work and education that leverages the power of storytelling. At E.O.I., blending and bottling wine are metaphors for exploring the challenges and triumphs of an organization's current state of affairs. It is a new style of educating the mind, heart, and will of tomorrow's leaders that may very well exceed all other previous techniques.

Commentary

The last sentence of Bruce's narrative reminds us that we must develop leaders' hearts, and wills; not just their minds. This totality of mind, heart, and will is an essential aspect of the bonding and healing power of stories. Over the last 15 years, there has been an emerging field of research called neurocardiology that studies the connections between the brain and the heart. According to researchers at the HeartMath Institute, there are more neural connections between the heart and the brain than there are within the brain itself. The institutes' researchers point out that our long-cherished Western, Cartesian emphasis on cognitive processes in describing intelligence is overstated. The heart and the gut are part of a system of intelligence. I was amazed to learn that during embryonic development there is a very early stage in which the undifferentiated cells that become the brain are connected to cells that already exhibit the beating characteristics of a heart, which is in turn connected to more cells that eventually differentiate into our stomach or gut.

Bruce's narrative paints the picture of a man dedicated to the pursuit of the key leadership virtues of awareness of self and awareness of others. Through his ability to reflect on his stories, he discovers the critical role they played in helping him build and sustain the relationships key to the winery's success. Today that passion guides his vision and work at E.O.I., where groups are invigorated by the alchemy of blending their unique stories and talents to succeed and personally thrive.

Part II / *Putting Stories to Work*

THUS FAR we have taken a conceptual look at how stories function. We started by examining three functions of stories that are central to communication: stories empower a speaker and create an environment, stories encode information, and stories are a tool for thinking. Expanding upon the essential role of stories in communication, we discussed two more functions of stories that are central to management: stories require active listening, and stories help us negotiate differences. Active listening is at the heart of stories. We established a central tenet of this book:

> *Elicit other people's stories and your own, actively listen to them, and you will improve communications and build satisfying, productive, rewarding relationships in all areas of your life.*

Part I concluded with an analysis of the role of stories in leadership. Relationships were shown to be the most important work of any leader. We looked at the association of awareness of self, awareness of others, and stories. Three functions of stories were discussed to understand this association: stories help people bond with one another, stories can be used as weapons, and stories can be used for healing.

The three chapters in Part II offer processes, tools, and exercises for using stories to improve communications and build relationships. Chapters 7 and 8 focus on individual techniques, and chapter 9 focuses on group techniques. Chapter 7 guides readers through a series of personal reflections aimed at developing a large collection of personal stories. Although they are presented sequentially, they do not have to be completed in any particular order. Take your time and be reflective.

Chapter 8 shows how to find the connections between your stories. The importance of indexing is explained. A technique I developed called story collaging is offered as a valuable tool for creating a strong index for putting stories to work.

Chapter 9 contains a collection of exercises intended to be used with groups. The chapter is divided into two sections. The first section contains guidelines and identifies practice opportunities on how to develop keener observational skills in organizations through stories. The second section of the chapter has 10 exercises that can be used in any type of workshop or meeting to help participants develop stronger story skills.

Concepts and theories are important, but Part II of this book is where the rubber meets the road. I invite you to experiment and really work with stories. Just being knowledgeable of how stories work in communication, managing, and leading will not make you more effective. You must roll up your sleeves and start working with stories all the time until it becomes second nature. I have only scratched the surface in terms of putting stories to work. This is where your journey can begin.

Please e-mail me at terrence@makingstories.net to share the insights you unearth along your way. With your permission, I'll pass along your discoveries to others through my Web site: http://www.makingstories.net.

7 / Building an Index of Personal Stories

THIS CHAPTER GUIDES readers through a series of personal reflections that can be used to understand how past experiences shape current perceptions, attitudes, beliefs, and behaviors. You may feel that your interactions at work are separate from your personal history, but that's not true. How you see the world is colored by experiences buried deep in your mind.

Going through these reflections will help elicit memories. Your task is to thoughtfully review them, analyze them, gain new insights, and index them for future use. Doing so will greatly improve your relationships at work. You will find that you are less likely to react passively to people and situations. Whatever is happening to you at any given moment at work or elsewhere will be processed by another layer of awareness that is the "story mind." The story mind considers possibilities and seeks to continually attach new shades of meaning and interpretation to the events it observes and reflects on.

In this chapter I occasionally use a personal example. I think it is inappropriate for me to ask you to examine your past without sharing a bit of mine. The examples are intended to be brief illustrations. Vulnerability plays in important role in putting stories to work to improve communications and build relationships. Being vulnerable allows us to be honest with ourselves and enhances our ability to connect more effectively with others. I share a few of my stories with you to serve as an example and to enhance my communication by making a personal connection.

Look beyond the face value of your stories. It's true that some of them will not be very significant. Perhaps they are brief memories. However, many of them will be significant, and if you examine them carefully, you will likely discover unexpected things. Our personal stories are loaded with layers of potential meaning. If we reflect on our stories, we will discover new lessons and develop new theories about the world and ourselves. Our personal stories help us feel more integrated. Instead of repeating undesirable patterns of thought and behavior, we will be more capable of adopting new ones. Furthermore, we will be able to recognize similar patterns and stories in others. Sharing our stories either through words or actions can help others find and tell their own stories to gain new insights.

NOTE ON HOW TO USE TABLE 7.1

For the sections later in this chapter on personal topics, use Table 7.1 to capture your stories. There are three columns in the table. Here is a breakdown of the columns and an explanation of how to use them.

1. *Description of story.* Use a few words or short phrases to record a brief recollection of the story.
2. *Trigger.* Write down a word or two that you associate with the story. It should help you quickly recall the story because it will be used to index your story. Indexing is a crucial step in tapping into the power of stories. Have you ever looked in someone's file drawer and wondered how he or she can find anything? Large quantities of information need to be indexed and require a good indexing system. As you explore your stories in this chapter, you will find a great deal of information in them, but if you do not have a way of accessing them quickly, they will be of little value. You must create your own indexing scheme. Trying to fit your experiences into someone else's indexing scheme does not work.
3. *Connection-relationship to other stories and possible applications.* Make a record of how the story relates or is connected to any others. It is very common for one story to trigger another one. Second, think about any insights you have gained from the story and about when you might share it with someone else.

Table 7.1

Description of Story	Trigger	Connection—relationship to other stories and possible applications

Here is an example. I start the process by recalling my personal stories.

1. There is a six-year age difference between my sister and me. The age difference didn't matter because we were very close and she spoiled me rotten. Although we didn't have a lot of money for material things, in terms of attention, love, and care, I was a spoiled brat. Regardless of what my sister was doing, she always tried to include me in her activities. If she and her friends were going roller-skating, Franca took me. If Franca's friends wanted to see a movie, she wouldn't go with them unless they agreed to let me tag along.

2. At an early age Franca instilled in me the spirit of entrepreneurship. We formed a company called DIACO (also known to its board of directors as Do It All Company). There was no task too big or too small for DIACO. If we could make a buck, we would do the job. We went around the neighborhood handing out our homemade business cards.

3. Franca was no stranger to hard work. I remember picking her up on Saturday and Sunday evenings after she had worked all day at the switchboard in the Santa Catalina High School office. She learned how to handle a variety of personalities and dynamics at a young age. Today people marvel at her people skills. Yet few people know all the sacrifices and hard work behind the qualities they admire so much.

4. Through her example, Franca taught me the value of hard work. I followed her lead, and when I went to a boarding high school, I also helped pay for my education by answering the switchboard, cleaning classrooms, and washing dishes on the weekends.

5. When it was time to go to college, finances did not deter Franca. She fulfilled her dream and went to Georgetown University. With a combination of scholarships, student loans, and a lot of work, Franca graduated in three and a half years.

6. Every step of the way Franca taught me how to dream and how to work hard to bring my dreams to life.

This example contains multiple stories, and it highlights many of the features we have discussed about stories. To begin with, there is not just one story here. There are six stories. As explained in chapter 1, stories do not need to be long; even a few words can be a story. Also notice how one story flows into the next. One story triggers another one, and all of the stories are interconnected.

In the second part of the example, we will use the chart shown in Table 7.2.

Table 7.2

Description of Story	Trigger	Connection—relationship to other stories and possible applications
1. Growing up with sister Franca 2. Being spoiled by her 3. Forming our company DIACO 4. Seeing her work hard. 5. Following in her footsteps during high school 6. Watching her realize her dream of going to Georgetown University	Sister Being spoiled Summer job High school Switchboard Dish washing Hard work Dream College	Share stories with young people who are working hard to achieve their dreams but who may feel for one reason or another discouraged Use stories to emphasize how long I have been working and how many experiences I have had along the way Story is related to some of the other following personal story topics: high school, sister, summer jobs, answering the switchboard, dish washing, college, hard work, sacrifices, and dreams

Personal Topic 1: Childhood (Up to Twelve Years Old)

It's so hard to remember the details of childhood. The years fly by, and yet many developmental psychologists assert that these are the most important and formative years of our lives. Who we are today is largely the result of early childhood experiences. Our childhood environment brings out many of our genetic predispositions. Many of our habits, thought patterns, perceptions of the world, and expectations of others are formed in these years.

Whether it was wonderful, painful, or just a blur, try to recapture any memory or sensation of your childhood that you can. Regardless of our age, we are all children at heart. Maybe you recall the simple pleasure of playing without any cares or concerns. When an activity becomes an end unto itself, this can cause people to feel a special sort of happiness. Perhaps this is the same happiness we long for and seek in our adult lives.

Questions to Guide You and Elicit Stories

What were your favorite toys?

How was your room decorated?

What games did you enjoy playing?

Did you have any stuffed animals?

Did you have an invisible or imaginary friend?

What were your favorite bedtime stories?

What were your favorite foods?

Were there any special events you always looked forward to?

Did you have any birthday parties?

Did you like to pretend to be a character or person?

Do you remember losing your first teeth? Did the tooth fairy visit you?

Were you ever seriously sick or injured during your childhood?

What was the most mischievous thing you ever did?

What got you into the most trouble?

Who was your best friend?

Did you have a lucky charm?

What was your favorite color?

What was your favorite song?

Did you have a nickname?

What was your favorite TV show?

What was your favorite movie?

Did you take music lessons?

What sports did you play?

Were you a member of any clubs?

Were you ever horribly mixed up or confused about any words or concepts?

Did you go away to camp?

Did you go on any family vacations?

Personal Topic 2: Parents and Siblings

Parents are truly a mystery. They have such a profound influence on us, but we are very different from them. We are an extension of them, but we are unique. Although we may have similar physical and emotional traits and characteristics, we are not identical to our parents or siblings. The mystery lies in sorting out how we creatively define ourselves. Parents and siblings are like mirrors. We can see reflections and aspects of ourselves in them. As we study them and our relationships with them, we are looking for signs and hints to help us understand our self-perceptions of our identity. How have we been affected by our parents? What parts of them are inside us? These are stories that can be rewritten. With our children, we try to build upon the strengths of our parents and identify areas in which we want to improve.

Questions to Guide You and Elicit Stories

What stories do you know about your parents' childhood?

What things did you do with your parents?

Do you have any memories of shopping for food or clothing with your parents?

Were you ever jealous of your siblings? Were they ever jealous of you?

What do you admire most about your parents?

What aspects of your relationship with your parents were difficult?

While you were growing up, were there any major events in your parents' lives?

Did you ever see your parents frightened?

How did your parents relate to one another?

Who were your parents' friends?

What hobbies or interests did your parents have?

What things upset your parents?

Did your parents give you chores?

Did you have an allowance?

How did your parents express affection?

How did your parents express anger?

Were you spoiled in any way?

Did you or any of your siblings receive special treatment?

Were your parents strict?

What sort of rules did you have while growing up?

Were your parents involved in the community?

What did your friends say and think about your parents?

Did your parents ever apologize to you?

In what ways did you try to please your parents?

What were some of the most memorable gifts your parents gave you?

How did your parents express disappointment?

What do you cherish most about your parents?

Personal Topic 3: Grandparents and Other Relatives

Although I never knew my grandparents, I feel a remarkable connection to my grandfather on my mother's side. He was hit by a car and killed when my mother was just a little girl, right around Christmas time. My grandmother was left with six children in the heart of the Depression. Everyone describes my grandfather as a jovial man. He loved to dance and sing. He also loved to sit around the dining room table telling stories while he carefully cut an apple or piece of fruit that he shared with the entire family. In fact, recently I inherited the old pocketknife he used to cut the fruit. Needless to say, it is a priceless memento. He has been a guardian in my life.

Many cultures recognize the importance of ancestors and have elaborate rituals associated with them. They become a crucial and omnipresent part of our lives. We learn about them through stories and personal items. We have a strange connection to the past. Maybe it's because we know parts of ourselves are locked up in a past we can only imagine and access through stories. Reflect on the role grandparents and relatives have played in your life and the stories you know about them.

Questions to Guide You and Elicit Stories

What were your grandparents' lives like?

When and how did your family come to America?

What stories have your parents told you about your grandparents?

What physical or personality characteristics do you share with any of your relatives?

What kind of work did your grandparents do?

What stories have your grandparents told you?

What stories have your other relatives told you?

Were your parents close to their parents? Have they always been close?

Were your parents close to any of their siblings? Have they always been close?

Have there been any family feuds?

How did your grandparents meet?

What mementos or family heirlooms do you have? What are the stories behind them?

If you have cousins, how was their childhood different from yours?

Do you have a special connection to any relative? How did it develop?

Do you dislike any of your relatives? How did those feelings develop?

Did any of your relatives serve in a war?

If they are dead, how did your grandparents die?

Have you seen anyone in your family suffer a serious illness?

Are there any forbidden topics or secrets in your family?

Whom do you admire most in your family?

Personal Topic 4: Pets and Animals

I did not have pets growing up. My mother always said she had enough "pets" to take care of with my sister, dad, and me. However, my father is a cat person. Without fail, if there is a cat nearby, it will walk up to my father. Even though we did not have pets, there was always some cat around that adopted my father. The most memorable of these was Leo. Leo lived with a clan of stray cats under the music building my father supervised on the military base of Fort Ord in Monterey, California. One night all these cats walked into the building. Leo moved out in front of the group and approached my father. He must have decided he liked my father because he turned on the other cats and sent them running out of the building. From that day on, whenever Leo heard the sound of my father's car, he ran out from under the building to greet my father and keep him company while he worked.

Today my father is a proud grandfather. Kirean, his "grandson," is a Maine Coon cat he inherited from me. (My role as cat owner was unsuccessful because I travel too much.) Now, even my mother sits Kirean on her lap and has what she calls "conversations" with him. It's amazing to see how much joy he brings to our family.

Why do pets affect us so deeply? Pets are used therapeutically and have been shown to improve the length and quality of people's lives. Not long ago, I saw a television interview with a little boy in which the interviewer asked him why pets do not live as long as people. The boy said it was because, as human beings, we spend our lives learning how to be kind and thoughtful toward others and that animals die sooner because they already know how to love. People love to tell stories about their pets. Whether you had a pet or not, take a minute to recall experiences you have had with and stories you have heard about animals and pets.

Questions to Guide You and Elicit Stories

What pets did you have while growing up?

How did your pets affect your family's life?

What are your feelings toward pets?

How would you describe your pets' personalities?

Were any of your pets closer to anyone else in your family?

What are some of the funny things your pets did?

What do you recall about the death of any of your pets?

How did you come up with your pets' names?

How did you get your pets?

Were your pets friendly with any neighborhood pets?

How did your pets act toward other people?

Did your pets have any favorite foods?

Where did your pets sleep?

What were your pets' favorite toys?

What were your pets' favorite games?

What animals are you afraid of?

What are your favorite animals?

What animal do you identify with the most?

Personal Topic 5: High School and Teenage Years

The teenage years can be tumultuous. We go through so many changes in a short time. We are not adults, but we are not children. We are stuck somewhere in between. We desperately want our independence but still require structure, discipline, and, most of all, tender care. What about the transition from middle school to high school? We go from the top of a pecking order to the bottom. How did you assert and define yourself during this period?

High school is a time of dealing with new friendships, activities, and decisions. Teenagers begin to develop strong ideas, values, and ideals to which they swear they will always adhere. As teenagers, we hear others say that these are the best years of our life, but we have little to compare them with. Senior year is either so perfect we never want it to end or it is troubled; but graduating and moving on to higher education is terrifying. Whatever the experience, teenage years are larger than life. Teens awaken to the world in new ways. They hunger to make their mark by finding and asserting their uniqueness in a confusing and often contradictory world.

Questions to Guide You and Elicit Stories

What do you remember about your first days of high school?

Were you a member of any clubs?

Were you on any athletic teams?

What was your daily routine like?

What were your favorite hangouts?

What was lunch like in the cafeteria?

Did you ever get into serious trouble?

Did you have any enemies?

Did you have a clique of friends?

Who were some of the memorable students, teachers, and school personalities?

Who were the most popular students?

Whom were you attracted to?

What experiences did you have dating?

Did you go on any class field trips?

What were the most difficult classes?

What classes did you like the most? The least?

What were your experiences with high school dances and parties?

How was your high school prom?

What jobs did you work?

Did you participate in any school shows or concerts?

What were your first experiences with alcohol or drugs?

Were you involved in any community activities?

What was your favorite music? Did you go to any concerts?

What did you wear to school?

What kind of student were you?

How was the college application process?

What mattered the most to you?

How did you spend your summers?

Personal Topic 6: College

I went to college at Brandeis University. The transition from the West Coast to the East Coast was dramatic. I had never seen the glorious metamorphosis of fall or played in the snow. I had gone to a boarding high school, so I was fairly accustomed to roommates and being on my own, but I was not thrilled to be in school. High school had tired me out, and even with scholarships and financial aid, the only way I could afford to go to school was by working 20 hours a week. I remember reading the list of "work study" jobs. I had washed dishes, cleaned classrooms, and answered telephones to help pay for high school. The thought of working in a cafeteria again repulsed me. In order to get a better-paying and more challenging job, I posed as a graduate student, hoping to be hired as a research assistant for a policy think tank. To impress my prospective employer, I walked into the interview carrying a briefcase. They knew I wasn't a graduate student, but they must have been impressed by my nerve and determination, because I got the job.

After all the standardized tests, essays, applications, college tours, and counseling, high school students are exhausted. It's a wonder they have the reserves to actually go to college. The first real taste of freedom usually comes during the college years. Maybe you traveled far away to another part of the country, or maybe your life did not change much at all. Perhaps you could attend college only part time. In my family, going to college was a big deal. My father never graduated from high school, and my mother longed to attend college but never did.

In college we are surrounded by diversity. We are challenged to go outside our comfort zones. We meet people with all sorts of experiences and with different ideas and values. We immerse ourselves in ideas and digest huge quantities of information. We develop elaborate social networks, and, most important, we add the finishing touches to identities we began creating in high school.

Questions to Guide You and Elicit Stories

How were your first days of college?

Who were your roommates?

How did you decide on your major?

What jobs did you have in college?

What activities were you involved in?

What kind of social life did you have?

Who were your friends?

What were the most difficult classes?

What classes did you like the most? The least?

What was the worst grade you ever got?

How did you cope with the pressure of finals?

How did you spend your vacations?

What kind of study habits did you have?

Did you ever cheat?

What did you do for your 21st birthday?

What changes did you undergo in college?

Who had the most influence on you?

What was the craziest thing you did?

What changes did you see in your friends?

What was the best paper you ever wrote?

What did you enjoy about college the most?

Personal Topic 7: Teachers and Mentors

Great teachers leave lasting impressions. They challenge us and change the way we see the world and ourselves. Perhaps they know how to push us, or maybe they see gifts, abilities, or potentials within us and refuse to let us sit back and not realize them. Maybe we are moved by their enthusiasm and love for teaching. Exceptional teachers know how to make learning fun. Somehow every lesson becomes a novel experience. They engage our minds and captivate our imaginations.

Mentors are special guides. Sometimes we find them, and sometimes they find us. They share their experiences and help us to focus on answering the right questions. Rarely do they give answers, but they offer their time, energy, and insights; the rest is up to us. Think about the impact teachers have had on you and the people who have played a major role in guiding you. Then consider how you are a teacher and mentor to others.

Questions to Guide You and Elicit Stories

Who were your favorite teachers?

Who were your least favorite teachers?

How would you describe their style of teaching?

How did they affect you?

How did they affect other students?

Did you ever tell them what impact they had on you?

Were you attracted to any of your teachers?

Did you receive special treatment from any teachers?

What did you learn from your teachers?

What do you know about your teachers' lives and experiences?

Did you ever disappoint any of your teachers?

Did any of them disappoint you?

Have you ever thought about being a teacher? If so, what subject would you want to teach?

What do you think about your children's teachers?

Were there any influential coaches in your life?

In what ways do you emulate your favorite teachers and mentors?

Did they have any favorite sayings or tidbits of wisdom?

How have your impressions of these teachers changed over the years?

Who were your mentors?

How did you meet them?

How did they help you?

How has the role of mentors in your life changed over the years?

Did you ever receive bad guidance from a mentor?

If you could have anyone as your mentor, who would it be? Why?

How are you a mentor to others?

Have you ever given bad guidance to others?

Do you feel compelled to help certain types of people? Why?

If you could spend a day in anyone's life, whose would it be?

Personal Topic 8: Stories Told to Me

It's magic, and I see it all the time: The moment I say the words "Once upon a time" or "Let me tell you a story," people's eyes light up, and I instantly have their attention. I recall bedtime stories with great pleasure. It was my favorite time of day; I was relaxed and tucked into bed, listening to the soothing sound of my mother's voice reading a story. I also recall running around on the playground working up a sweat during afternoon recesses and coming back to the classroom to lay my head on my desk and listen to my third-grade teacher read aloud from a book. We protested loudly every time she stopped.

We always love hearing stories, but it's interesting to take note of which ones stand out in our minds. Which ones do we remember and why do we remember them? Stories are hidden containers for our thoughts, hopes, beliefs, and fears. Reflecting on the stories that were told to us can help open emotional containers we may not realize are there. Think back on all the stories you were told and what role they play in your psyche today.

Questions to Guide You and Elicit Stories

What stories left the greatest impression on you?

What is the first story told to you that you remember?

What stories did you love to hear over and over again?

What stories captivated you the most?

What stories did you never believe?

What stories did you repeat to others?

What family stories were told to you?

What's the scariest story you ever heard?

What's the most uplifting story you ever heard?

Are there any stories you have tried to forget but have been unable to?

What stories did your parents tell about you?

What stories mean the most to you?

What stories angered you?

Did you feel compelled to research any stories told to you? If so, which ones and why?

How have you adapted or changed any stories told to you?

What religious stories were told to you?

Which religious stories had the greatest impact on you?

What stories did your teachers tell you?

What stories did your friends tell you?

What is the most recent story that stands out in your mind?

What story or story character best describes you?

Personal Topic 9: Friends

We give our hearts to friends and we entrust them with our secrets. They are there in good times, and they are there to help us through our darkest moments. Often they pass in and out of our lives, or we lose touch with them. Sometimes we have a falling out, or what may have started as an instantaneous and strong connection just fizzles. Perhaps we go long periods of time without seeing or speaking to friend, but it has no effect on the strength of the relationship.

We have many associates with whom we interact socially or professionally, but we consider only a few people to be close friends. Friends are so many things. Different friends fill different needs. One friend may be light-hearted and fun, and another may be thoughtful and serious. One we go to in a time of need, and another one we go to in a time of joy. Friends are reflections of different aspects of our selves. Have you ever heard the saying, "Show me your friends, and I will tell you who you are?" Take some time to think about the roles friends have played in your life.

Questions to Guide You and Elicit Stories

Who were your childhood friends? How did you meet them?

Who were your friends in high school? How did you meet them?

Who were your friends in college? How did you meet them?

What sort of mischief did you get into with your friends?

What were the strengths of these relationships?

How did the relationships change over time?

Did your parents dislike any of your friends? Why?

Who are your friends now? How did you meet?

Who is your closest friend? Why do you consider him or her your closest friend?

What were some of the worst fights you had with friends?

Have you ever lost a friend?

Have you ever had a falling out with a friend?

Have you ever intentionally hurt a friend?

Have you ever unintentionally hurt a friend?

Have you been jealous of any of your friends?

Have your friends been jealous of you?

What interests and activities did (do) you share with your friends?

What are some of the most memorable things friends have done for you?

How have you helped your friends?

Have you ever received bad advice from a friend?

Have you ever given bad advice to a friend?

Are there things you wish you had confided to a friend?

How have your friendships changed you as a person?

Personal Topic 10: Disappointments and Betrayal

Disappointments can be devastating. When someone makes a promise to us, we expect it to be fulfilled. Promises are shadows of the elusive certainty we long for in our lives. The future cannot all be unknown; shouldn't there be some things we can count on? As children, it could be the excitement of knowing our parents are going to take us somewhere, do something with us, or get us something.

Disappointments hurt on both sides. I will never forget a valuable lesson in disappointment that I learned from my sixth-grade teacher, Mrs. Lutz. She really believed in me. She encouraged me to participate in the Daughters of the American Revolution essay contest, which I won at the school, local, regional, and state levels. After that I began to tread on her confidence in me by handing in poor and late homework assignments. She made it quite clear that she was disappointed in me and that I had violated her trust. To know that you have disappointed someone is a horrible feeling. Disappointments come in all shapes and sizes, but betrayals are the worst. Of course, one cannot have trust without the possibility of betrayal. The two go hand in hand. However, our world is turned upside down when someone betrays us. Trusting makes us vulnerable. Any time we make ourselves vulnerable we can easily be hurt. We must hope that betrayals do not harden us or make us reluctant to trust others or ourselves.

Questions to Guide You and Elicit Stories

What promises have been made to you and broken?

What promises have you made and broken?

Were any of your teachers ever disappointed in you?

Did you ever disappoint your parents?

How have your friends disappointed you?

How have you disappointed your friends?

How have you disappointed your spouse?

What are some of the ways you have disappointed your children?

How have you disappointed yourself?

When have you felt betrayed in your life?

What lies have you told your friends?

What lies have you told your family?

What lies have you told your colleagues?

In what ways have you broken the trust of your friends?

In what ways have you broken the trust of your spouse?

In what ways have you broken the trust of someone in your family?

Have you been able to regain the trust of these people? If so, how?

What ideas have you believed in strongly?

Have you been disappointed by the failure of any of your ideas?

What causes have you been involved in?

In what ways were you disappointed by any of these causes or ideals?

What events in your life have made you distrustful in any way?

What events in your life have made you cynical in any way?

Personal Topic 11: First Love

How can we forget the overwhelming feelings of falling in love for the first time? The world becomes a magical place. We are convinced that we are destined to be the next great romantic couple, and we vow never to let anything get between us. Sometimes we marry our first love. Sometimes the failure of a first love forces us to grow painfully in ways we could have never imagined. Whatever the experience, we are never the same.

I was always prone to schoolboy crushes, and even in grade school I was a flirt. My first great love was Kveta (or Tuska, as her family and friends affectionately called her). I met her at the end of my senior year in college. Her beautiful long blond hair, distinctive facial features, and sharp intellect captivated my imagination. It began as innocent flirting, but in no time our mutual interests and values sparked a powerful connection. We spent two summers completely absorbed in each other. We did everything together, and our activities ran the gamut from painting her family's farmhouse, cooking lavish meals, going to museums and concerts, hiking, and fencing to giving free piano and singing concerts at nursing homes.

We spent the rest of these two years apart from each other. One year I was in Hungary doing research on a fellowship, and the second year Tuska spent her junior year of college studying in Germany. We wrote long notes and journal entries to each other almost every day that we were apart. But we never made it to our third summer. Eventually distance and the process of growing in different directions doused our flames. Although the breakup was painful, I treasure the time we spent with each other. That first love prepared me for future ones. Love may be our greatest calling. To have not loved is a great tragedy. Think back upon your experiences with love, and try to understand how they have changed you.

Questions to Guide You and Elicit Stories

How did you meet your first love?

What attracted you to him or her?

What did your friends and family think about your first love?

How did your relationship end?

What was your first sexual experience like?

Has anyone ever broken your heart?

Have you ever broken anyone's heart?

Have you experienced unrequited love?

How did your experiences of first love change your beliefs about love?

Have you ever fallen in love but been unable to act on your feelings?

Who are some of the people you dated?

What did you find most attractive about these people?

Have any of these people remained your friends?

How did you meet your spouse?

What kind of things did you do together while you were dating?

What experiences have helped your marital relationship evolve?

Have you ever been divorced? What things brought about failure of the marriage?

Have you ever been tempted to cheat on your spouse?

Personal Topic 12: The Hardest Things

Life is not easy. Every stage of life has challenges. Even our first moment of life is difficult. To an unsuspecting infant, leaving the womb and taking his or her first breath of air is a huge undertaking. Sometimes it seems as if problems follow us like dark clouds, never leaving us alone, and never letting us get too comfortable with who and how we are.

No matter how much we may be at ease in one situation, there are always new ones waiting to push us to our limits. An athlete, for example, learns how to respect the limits of his or her body and mind but also never assumes that those limits cannot be pushed. Or take the example of pioneers. They know the benefits of charting new territories, and they realize that the status quo is not always acceptable. They are unwilling to let complacency and stagnation rule the day. Athletes and pioneers may be at the extreme end of the spectrum, but what we can learn from them is that the most difficult challenges are the ones that help us grow the most.

Perhaps there was a phase of your life that was difficult. How did you cope with the pressures it generated? Maybe your family moved, and you were uprooted from all your friends, or maybe your parents got divorced. Perhaps it was a subject in school or a transition you underwent in your life. We do not want to dwell on the hard things, but we want to be aware of how they have challenged us and helped us to stretch in new directions.

Questions to Guide You and Elicit Stories

What challenges are you facing in your life now?

What are some of the hardest things you have ever had to do?

What are some of the hardest things you have ever had to say to someone?

Have there been difficult situations that you have avoided in your life?

Are there any hard things you are afraid to attempt?

What hard things have you attempted to do but failed?

How have you coped with the difficult challenges in your life?

What has been the hardest phase of your life?

How have others helped you?

How have others pushed you to tackle hard things?

What is the hardest lesson you have ever learned?

What are the difficult things that you have done that have surprised you?

What have been some of the greatest obstacles to achieving your goals?

Personal Topic 13: Time in the Spotlight

I have always been a ham. I can remember the thrill I felt in kindergarten when I had the only speaking part as the head elf in the Christmas play. That first experience of being in the spotlight hooked me.

Success is sweet. Both introverts and extroverts love to be recognized and appreciated by others. Every person is unique and has special gifts. Sooner or later, a time comes when our gifts and experiences are needed. Contributing them affirms our identity and reminds us that we are special. Perhaps the spotlight shines on us not so much for other people to see us but for us to see ourselves more clearly.

Spotlights are not always large and bright. Sometimes a simple compliment or passing remark leaves us glowing for days. What about those times when you thought you deserved to be in the spotlight and somehow someone else stole the attention and recognition you deserved? Or maybe you were in the spotlight for doing something negative.

Many people tend to downplay their successes or feel that they are insignificant compared to the successes of others. But we need to keep our trophies polished and on display. Knowing our success stories gives us strength and enables us to appreciate and recognize the contributions of others. Take this time to recall your successes.

Questions to Guide You and Elicit Stories

What awards have you won during your life?

What is one of the greatest compliments you have ever received?

What achievements are you the most proud of?

How did being in the spotlight affect your behavior?

Have you ever been in the spotlight and felt that you didn't deserve it?

Have you ever felt that someone stole the spotlight from you?

Have you done something for which you wanted recognition but never received it?

Have you ever been featured in a newspaper article? On the radio? Television?

Have you ever purposely given the spotlight to someone else?

Have you ever gone out of your way to try to be popular?

When have you been the center of attention?

Have you been jealous of others in the spotlight?

Have you been in the spotlight for something negative?

What have been your greatest professional accomplishments?

What do people admire most about you?

What talents or gifts do you possess that you treasure the most?

What are some of the ways in which you have recognized the talents and contributions of others?

Personal Topic 14: Death

Nothing fully prepares us for death. Yet we can be sure: we are going to die, and everyone who is important to us will die. It is the nature of things.

When we are young we are sure that we are invincible. Death is the furthest thing from our minds. Somewhere along the line, death shows its face for the first time. I remember my first two experiences with death. I was about eight years old when I found a dead newborn kitten. I was paralyzed and overcome with intense sadness. I thought to myself, How could something so innocent and so fragile die? I buried the kitten and conducted an elaborate ceremony for it, but the image of the lifeless kitten haunted me for a long time. A couple of years later, one of my father's sisters died. My mother tried to prepare me for what I would see and feel at the funeral. But nothing could possibly have prepared me for the sight of my father crying uncontrollably.

Life is fragile and impermanent. If everything else is a moving target, at least death punctuates our lives with certainty. The inevitability of death arouses a desire to leave our mark on the world; we want to make sure we will be remembered. And that is what stories guarantee us.

Take a moment to reflect on how death has touched your life.

Questions to Guide You and Elicit Stories

What was your first encounter with death?

Have you ever been in a life-threatening situation?

How was death described to you as a child?

Have any of your friends died?

Have you watched any of your friends deal with death?

Did you see your parents deal with death?

When did you realize your parents would die someday?

When was the first time you realized that you would die someday?

Have you spent much time in hospitals?

Have you ever seen someone die?

Have you watched an animal die or suffer?

How have you explained death to your children?

How has aging affected you? Your friends? Your family?

What do you think death is like?

Do you believe in life after death?

Personal Topic 15: Acts of Generosity

Regardless of how independent we think we are or want to be, we need the help of others. Our lives are inextricably interconnected. Look at any object near you and think about all the stories it represents. For example, take your car. Can you picture how your car was designed and all of the people, technology, and know-how it took to create it? What about the gas in your car's tank? Where did it come from? How did it get processed? Everything we have and everything we can do are the result of elaborate interdependent relationships. Like it or not, we need each other to survive.

Our first encounter with generosity comes from our parents. Whatever your experience has been, it is likely that we can never repay our parents for all of the time, energy, and care they have given us. Parents are not perfect, but most of them make sacrifices and shower their children with acts of love and generosity.

Throughout our lives, we encounter people who help us in unexpected ways. Sometimes help comes in the form of major acts, and sometimes it comes in a less elaborate form in the simple things people say or do for us. I am always touched by the generosity and hospitality people show me when I travel. People are proud of where they live, and they enjoy sharing the uniqueness of their place.

Giving to other people and being generous makes us feel good about ourselves. There is something wonderful, and perhaps altogether human, about helping others. Try to remember when people have been generous to you and the ways you have been generous to others.

Questions to Guide You and Elicit Stories

How have people been generous to you?

What's the most generous thing you have ever done?

What's the most generous thing you have seen someone else do?

How have people helped you when you have been traveling?

What generous things did you see your parents do for others?

How have your friends been generous to you?

At work, how have people been generous to you?

At work, how have you been generous to others?

Have there been times when you have failed to be generous?

Have there been times when you have not accepted someone's act of generosity?

Are you actively involved in your community?

What acts of generosity have you performed that are memorable?

Personal Topic 16: Hurt and Pain

We like to forget painful experiences. Pain can take many different forms. It can be physical, emotional, or psychological. Pain may not be desirable, but it plays an important role in our lives.

Physical pain ensures that we are in touch with the healing needs of our bodies. We have learned from our bodies that if we ignore pain, matters only get worse. In this way, pain is a blessing in disguise. It is a symptomatic indication of something that is more pressing and that requires our care. We must attend to our pains; otherwise they will turn into haunting demons.

We should not bury our pains, but instead should transform them into new lessons learned. We can be deepened by our experiences with pain. Everyone suffers in one way or another. It is a common part of the human experience. Others can benefit from our struggles. By being in touch with our painful experiences, we can be more attuned to the pain and suffering of others. It is a powerful experience to look into someone's eyes and understanding what he or she is feeling and going through. Our experiences with pain allow us to reach out to others. However, we must first look within ourselves to examine our own hurts and pains.

Questions to Guide You and Elicit Stories

Have you ever been seriously injured?

What things in your life have caused you pain?

How have other people hurt you?

Was there a time of your life that was painful?

How did you get through these painful times?

Have you ever tried to purposely hurt someone?

Has anyone gone out of his or her way to hurt you?

What painful experiences have you seen other people go through?

What hurtful things have people said to you?

How have you hurt other people with your words?

In what ways has your failure to say or do something hurt someone?

What pain do you fear most?

What pains have you seen your family endure?

How have you helped others in their times of pain?

Do you have any painful memories that are unresolved?

Personal Topic 17: Unfairness

"Who said life was fair?" Life is filled with injustices. I'll never forget one of my first experiences with unfairness. When I was about eleven years old, I entered the Monterey County Fair children's talent show. I decided to sing "Tie a Yellow Ribbon Round the Ole Oak Tree." I worked up a whole routine, complete with dancing. There was only one problem. At the last minute, my father had to work and could not play the piano for me. Determined not to let that dampen my act, I decided to do my routine without accompaniment. All humility aside, I brought the house down, but the judges gave me second place. First place went to a cute brother-and-sister dance team. The local television station obviously felt I had been treated unfairly, because they aired most of my routine on the evening news and did not even mention the winning team.

It's a harsh awakening when we realize that many things in life are not fair. We thirst for justice. The younger we are, the more steadfastly we cling to some ideal of justice. Plato was onto something when he defined justice as "the having and doing of what is one's own." For Plato, justice is fluid. In other words, no set of rules will ever adequately capture all circumstances or exigencies. We come to realize gradually that equality is sometimes achieved through inequality. Take a moment to reflect on all the unfairness you have experienced. How have you dealt with these experiences? Are there any ways in which you perpetuate injustices you have experienced?

Questions to Guide You and Elicit Stories

Have you ever cheated?

Has anything ever been stolen from you?

Have you been adversely affected by other people's cheating?

Have you ever been wrongfully accused?

As a child, were you ever punished for something you didn't do?

Have you ever felt discriminated against?

Have you discriminated against anyone?

What injustices have you witnessed?

When have you benefited from preferential treatment?

In what ways did your parents treat you unfairly?

Are there any ways in which you have been treated unfairly at work? Were you ever treated unfairly by any of your teachers?

Personal Topic 18: Moments of Joy and Pleasure

I hope memories of joy and pleasure come rushing to mind quickly. These are our treasures. In times of pain, hardship, doubt, or fear we can recall warm, happy memories to comfort ourselves and be reminded that things can and will get better.

Joys and pleasures come in many different forms and flavors. There are simple joys of relishing a beautiful day or the company of a good friend. Joys also come from accomplishing difficult goals. If we disengage the distracting and often negative droning of our minds, we discover a world filled with wonders, joys, and pleasures.

Questions to Guide You and Elicit Stories

What gives you pleasure?

What have been some memorable and joyful events in your life?

When have you been the happiest?

What was the happiest moment in your life?

What accomplishments have been pleasurable?

In what ways have you shared your joy with others?

What activities do you enjoy?

How have you spent time enjoying nature?

In what ways have music and art brought pleasure to you?

In what ways has your family been a source of joy?

What have been the special times you have enjoyed with your spouse?

How do you seek joy in your life?

Personal Topic 19: Holidays

Holidays are special times. Our daily routines are interrupted by special occasions. We usually share holidays with a community, but even if we spend a holiday by ourselves, we realize that we are connected to others who are also observing the holiday. Holidays can be religious or secular, but either way they uniquely focus our attention.

Usually there are traditions associated with holidays. Perhaps these are things we say, do, or eat. These traditions provide us with continuity. We look forward to these traditions because they ground us and give our lives structure.

How have you celebrated holidays, and what have they meant for you? As you think about your stories, be sure to include holidays such as birthdays and summer vacations.

Questions to Guide You and Elicit Stories

What are your favorite holidays?

What holiday traditions did your family have?

Were there special foods or rituals?

Are there any family heirlooms or objects associated with any of the holidays?

How have your holiday traditions changed over the years?

Do any of the holidays have religious significance for you?

How did you learn religious stories associated with holidays?

What were some of your most memorable holidays?

How have you celebrated national holidays indicative of your cultural background?

Have you ever been alone on a holiday?

How did you celebrate some of your birthdays?

How did you spend summer holidays?

Did your family go on vacations?

Have you ever been disappointed on a holiday?

Personal Topic 20: Food and Memorable Meals

Food is a glorious thing. Growing up in an Italian family, where eating was a central part of our daily life, has given me a keen appreciation for food. Eating is a sensuous activity. I am always saddened when I meet people who consider eating to be a chore. There are a finite number of meals in one's life, and my motto is to make the most of each one. What role does food play in your life? We all have likes and dislikes. How did you develop some of your current preferences?

Preparing and sharing meals with family and good friends is one of the most pleasurable activities in my life. When I am not involved in preparing or consuming a meal, I love to banter with other culinary aficionados. Meals often feature prominently in celebrations of special occasions, yet a meal does not have to be elaborate to be memorable. I can recall the pleasures of basking in the sun immersed in deep conversation with a good friend while consuming a loaf of bread, a tomato, some cheese, and some chocolate.

What meals have been memorable for you? Think beyond scrumptious food. Memorable meals can be much more than that. They include intimate conversations, dear friends, family, romantic interludes, momentous occasions, or the joys of exploring a new country.

Questions to Guide You and Elicit Stories

What are some of your favorite foods?

When and how were you introduced to these foods?

What did you like to eat as a child?

How did you develop some of your current food preferences?

Are there certain foods you will not eat? If so, why?

Have you ever gotten food poisoning?

Are you allergic to any foods? If so, when and how did you discover this?

Do you have any memories of going food shopping with your parents?

What have been some of the most memorable meals you have prepared?

How did you discover some of your favorite restaurants?

Have you ever gone to great lengths to find a particular food?

Do you recall any particular conversations that took place over a meal?

Did you ever make any important decisions during a meal?

While traveling, what have been some of your most memorable meals?

Personal Topic 21: Cars and Homes

Cars have made the world a smaller and more accessible place. Cars give us mobility and a sense of freedom. As kids, we long for that freedom, and cars make it possible. Was learning to drive a thrill for you? How about your first car? Think about the roles cars have played in your life and some of your memories associated with them.

Our home should be a sanctuary, a peaceful haven that provides comfort and warmth. At some point, most people long to build a secure nest. We endeavor to create a space that expresses who we are. We may have lived in many homes, and each of them is a rich source of memories. Where we have lived and the conditions in which we have lived shape our attitudes about the meaning of home. Maybe it's a first apartment or the first time living on one's own. Perhaps we have vivid memories of neighborhoods we have lived in. Visualize all of the places you have lived, and take a tour of the emotional landscape of home.

Questions to Guide You and Elicit Stories

How was the process of learning to drive?

Did you like to drive fast?

What are the stories behind any speeding tickets or moving violations you may have gotten?

What was the first car you bought?

What was your favorite car? Why?

When have your cars broken down?

Have you ever run out of gas?

What road trips have you gone on?

Do you have memories of driving in storms or bad weather?

Did you cruise around with your friends?

Did you go to drive-in movies?

Have you ever been in an accident?

What do you remember about the house(s) you lived in as a child?

How were these houses decorated?

What are some of your fondest memories about these houses?

Do you have any bad or sad memories associated with these houses?

What do you remember about the neighborhood(s) where you grew up?

Who were some of the more memorable people in your neighborhood?

When did you move out of your family's house?

What places have you lived in over the years?

Have you ever lived on your own?

What has been your favorite place? Why?

What influenced you to decorate your house today the way you have?

What are some of the key possessions in your house today that make it special for you?

Are there any special stories about how you acquired these things?

Personal Topic 22: Books and Movies

I still remember walking into the Monterey Public Library for the first time. I was fascinated by the shelves of books all around. Each book was an adventure, and I wanted to devour them all. Reading is such a joy. I am reminded of a TV episode of the *Twilight Zone* that featured a banker with horn-rimmed glasses who wanted only to sit, unperturbed, in the bank's vault and read. There was a nuclear attack and everyone in the town was killed except for him. Being in the bank vault saved his life. The lonely, distraught banker wanders through the decimated town until he stumbles upon the library. The final image of the episode shows him with an expression of complete happiness because he is finally able to read in unperturbed peace. As he reaches for a book, his glasses slide down his nose and shatter into pieces.

Certain books or movies resonate in special ways. Often we can better relate to our own challenges and dilemmas by vicariously working them out through the characters in books or movies. Sometimes a book or movie may simply whisk us away to far-off places and fantastic adventures.

What books and movies stand out in your mind? How do the characters and situations relate to you? What attracts you to these books and movies? Are there any common themes to these books and movies? If so, what aspects of your life are encoded in these themes?

Questions to Guide You and Elicit Stories

What were some of your favorite books growing up? Why?

What are some of your favorite books now? Why?

What parts of the books did you like the most?

Were there certain books that have meant more to you at certain times?

What was the first movie you ever saw?

Who are some of your favorite characters from books or movies?

If you could enter any book or movie, which would you choose? Why?

If you could be any characters from any book or movie, who would you choose to be?

What characters do you identify with the most?

Has anyone ever likened you to or compared you with a character from a book or movie?

If you were to write a book, what would it be about?

If you were to make a movie, what would it be about?

8 / Story Collaging

THIS CHAPTER OFFERS ideas on how to find the connections between stories. Stories in isolation are like islands without bridges—they are of limited value to us or anyone else. Stories are triggered by shared conversations about experiences and are resuscitated on the basis of an index. A rich index that is well cross-indexed increases the likelihood of finding a meaningful story when needed. Sharing stories spontaneously in the right situation and at the right time is a key practice of putting stories to work. And spontaneity with telling stories is a product of preparation and reflection. A jazz musician may make improvisational music look easy, but it takes long hours of study and practice to produce the illusion of ease; stories are no different.

Roger Schank (1995) describes the importance of indexing and its relationship to intelligence this way:

> Stories are everywhere, but not all stories look like stories. If you consider a story to be a previously prepared gist of something to say, something that you have said before or heard another say, then a great deal of conversation is simply mutual storytelling. Moreover, if the majority of what we say is in our memories in the form of previously prepared stories, the way we look at the nature of understanding and what it means to be intelligent must change. Is being very intelligent just having a great many stories to tell? Is it adapting superficially irrelevant stories into relevant ones, i.e., finding a story in one domain and applying it by analogy to another? Maybe it means combining stories and making generalizations from them or, perhaps intelligence is embodied in the initial process of collecting stories to tell in the first place. (pp. 26–27)

Schank suggests that intelligence is not defined by the collection or storage of a lot of information, but rather by the ability to index experiences in multiple ways and by the capacity for discovering the relationships between experiences in different domains. The hallmark of intelligence is the ability to collect stories and regularly reflect on them to continually gain new insights.

The previous chapter described a process to develop a collection of personal stories. This is the foundation. Now we need to develop an index for these stories, ferret out major themes from them, and look for interrelationships between them. The ability to connect stories in new ways gives them a renewed life and enables the opportunity to continuously learn from them. Our stories become fertile fields for personal reflections, templates for new learning, rich coffers of material for communications, and the basis on which relationships are built and sustained.

INTRODUCTION TO STORY COLLAGING

In my work with organizations I have developed a technique called Story Collaging. It is a form of brainstorming with stories. The idea is to take isolated stories and discover the connections between them. Here's how it works:

1. Start with a *story circle.* An example of a story circle would be any of the personal topics listed in the last chapter to elicit stories. The story circle is the unifying theme for all of the stories to be contained within it. It acts as the subject or operating domain for story brainstorming.
2. For each of the stories, create *story hubs*—descriptions of the stories and triggers or words that you associate with the story and that stimulate your recall of it.
3. Look at all the story hubs and build an index that ties the story hubs to one another.
4. Connect story circles to one another by finding relationships between story hubs from one or more story circles.

Putting stories to work demands that we have command of our stories. They need to be readily available when we need to communicate with others or learn from ourselves. Story Collaging, as with any form of brainstorming, is the first step in facilitating an individual's or group's process of unearthing insights. Story collages can be used in a variety of ways. Below are two examples. The first story collage helped me write a letter to my son about the nature of work and my attitudes toward it.

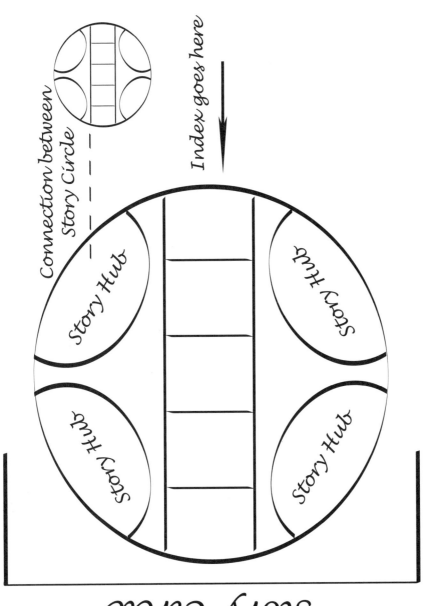

Connection between
Story Circle

Index goes here

Story Hub

Story Hub

Story Hub

Story Hub

Story Circle

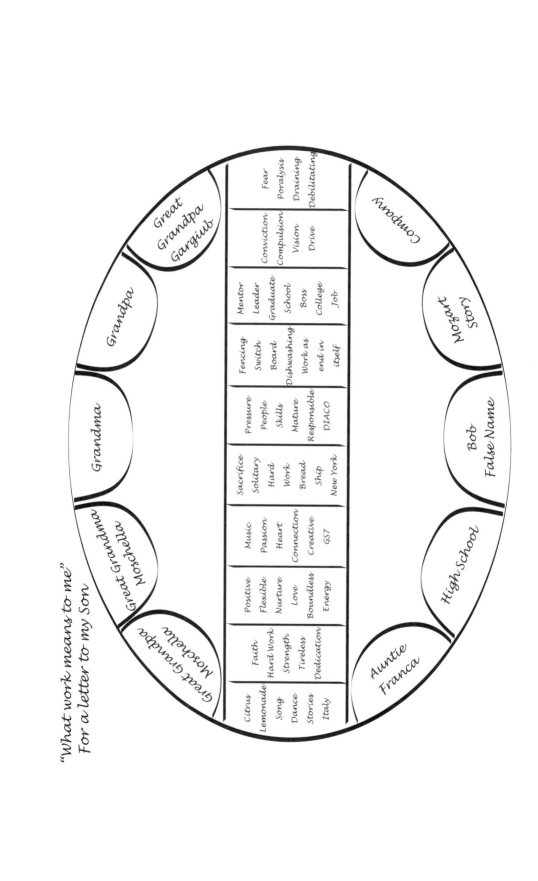

"What work means to me"
For a letter to my Son

Great Grandpa Moschella

Great Grandma Moschella

Grandma

Grandpa

Great Grandpa Gargiub

Auntie Franca

High School

Bob False Name

Mozart Story

Company

| Citrus Lemonade Song Dance Stories Italy | Faith Hard Work Strength Tireless Dedication | Positive Flexible Nurture Love Boundless Energy | Music Passion Heart Connection Creative GS7 | Sacrifice Solitary Hard Work Bread Ship New York | Pressure People Skills Mature Responsible DIACO | Fencing Switch Board Dishwashing Work as end in itself | Mentor Leader Graduate School Boss College Job | Conviction Compulsion Vision Drive | Fear Paralysis Draining Debilitating |

Sample Collage #1: Letter to My Son about Work

Work offers an infinite number of possibilities. It is first and foremost an expression of who and how we are. I want to share with you a collage of experiences. Through them I hope you will garner some insights. If there is one central to theme to all of the stories, it is this: may your work always bless you with opportunities to create, and may it always enable you to realize your full potential by constantly challenging you to grow, stretch, and learn.

My collage must begin with some context. My relationship to work has been shaped by generations of stories. Some persist as faint images, and others have a driving emotional persistence that is unwavering. Great-grandpa Gargiulo was a small man with Napoleonic determination. Coming to America was a mistake, the result of a self-imposed mutiny when one evening Great-grandpa's rolling pin, which should have been resting in the galley, became a tool for self-defense against the ship's captain instead of the bread he was known for. Marooned on Manhattan, Great-grandpa opened a bread bakery. Grandpa watched his father slave day and night. He helped in whatever ways he could; however, a certain sadness overshadowed Grandpa's admiration of his father's art. It was a hard life of physical labor, long nights, and often minimal family contact. The occasional outing to Coney Island was a treasured but rare treat. When the Great Depression hit and everything had been lost, Grandpa knew he was heading in a different direction.

Music moves Grandpa's soul. His vocation was to be found in notes, not with flour and yeast. He borrowed his father's passionate Neapolitan temperament and directed it in a new way. A melodious parade of harmonies and rhythms led him to the podium. Tantalizing, larger-than-life dramas pulsed through his veins. He discovered the joy of work. Grandpa lived and breathed opera—it took over every fiber of his being. There was no separation between work and life. His life was music. I have watched his magic time and again, and I am amazed by his immersion into a flow of sound and emotion. Four hours of a performance collapse into a point of singularity. Grandpa emerges from a trance, oblivious to the passage of time. I continue to chase after this otherworldly relationship to work, and I have found my own ways to cultivate it. Grandpa had his struggles too; we all do. Providence did not always grant Grandpa the musical elixir his soul longed for. Work brought its drudgery and bared its mundane head. Life as a GS7 (government services) in army music and recreation centers conjured many dark nights of doubt and frustration. Like a wizard robbed of his wand and incapable of magic, my father's absent baton ate away at his heart. However, necessity steadies our dour times and we lash our sense of purpose onto whatever life rafts we can find. Love for family was solace and nurturance in lean times.

Dedication, faith, and family were the cornerstones of Grandma's parents' orientation to work. Great-grandpa Francesco Moschella died when Grandma was a little girl. He left the citrus groves of southern Italy to pursue a new life in America. With minimal English and no education, Great-grandpa worked on the shipping docks of New York and any other odd jobs he could find. He was a man of song, dance, and stories. Each moment was a sacred game, and he adhered to only one rule: make joy in whatever you do. He saw every lemon of a situation as lemonade in disguise. Great-grandma raised a family of six by herself during the Depression. Her work was never ending. She was not daunted by life's exigencies. She found her purpose by giving completely of herself. Anything and everything was an opportunity to imbue it with care and indefatigable energy.

Grandma admired her mother's strength and independence. These are qualities she inculcated in all areas of her life and that she modeled for your Aunt Franca and me. Like Grandpa, Grandma was drawn to music. Juggling a job at Tiffany's, Grandma worked on the side as a singer. Her involvement in singing eventually led her to the baton of Maestro Gargiulo, and the rest is history. Change blows us in a wild myriad of directions. The glamour of singing for princes at high-society New York events, maintaining a studio at Carnegie Hall, and helping my father climb the world of opera dissolved into stints in Columbus, Ohio, Georgia, and eventually Monterey, California. Music took a back seat, and raising a family on virtually pennies became Grandma's focus.

Aunt Franca and I were possessed with an entrepreneurial drive. DIACO (Do It All Company) opened its doors for business the summer of my sixth year. Since Aunt Franca was six years older and wiser it was only appropriate to give her the helm of the company while I accepted a position on the board as chief operating officer. No job was out of our realm. When we weren't walking dogs, cleaning yards, or going shopping for the elderly, we were busy strategizing. We learned to dream and developed the capacity to see everything as possible. Those early childhood forays into business prepared me for my induction into the serious necessities of work. I watched Franca work her way through high school answering the school's switchboard on weekends. I saw her natural people skills blossom under the pressures of needing to be so mature and responsible for her age. I followed suit. To pursue my passion for fencing, I had to leave my hometown because I had outgrown my coach, and I had to go away to high school in order to train with the Olympic coach. Boarding school offered me a smorgasbord of jobs. From working the switchboard like Aunt Franca, cleaning classrooms, and washing dishes on the weekends, I began to see hard work not as a curse but as an end in itself. I suppose I didn't have any other choice.

By the time I arrived at university, I was exhausted. Even with scholarships and financial aid, I needed to work 20 hours a week. The list of jobs for underclassmen was horrifying. I felt I had already paid my dues working in kitchens, so I opted for a different strategy. I put on my best clothes, armed myself with a briefcase to project an air of mature professionalism, and walked over to the school's most prestigious think tank that was hiring a graduate student to work as a research assistant. Somehow I got the job.

Before I continued my tenure as an independent entrepreneur with my sister, I tackled stints as an employee. This meant facing bosses and authority structures. As such, these did not bother me. However, bosses can be strange beasts because of our relationships with them. Some of this is due to the positional power they hold. Most of it is a function of the psychological parental role we assign them. Bob FalseName was no exception. When I interviewed for the position of research assistant as a college freshman, he looked past my age and inexperience and saw my potential.

Over the next four years, Bob took me under his wings and became a wonderful mentor. Graduation from university offered me a hiatus in the form of a fellowship in Hungary, but when I returned a year later Bob made sure a job was waiting for me. During my first year of employment, Bob continued to act as my mentor and even pushed me to go to graduate school. I was given a tremendous amount of latitude to help the organization achieve its objectives. It was an invigorating time.

And then the inevitable happened. Bob became more human and vulnerable. I discovered he was not a perfect boss. He had fears like the rest of us. As the organization was going through some growing pains, he had very negative impacts on the people around him. Being a part of the organization, I lost sight of his humanness and became preoccupied with the organization's needs and what role I thought I could play in improving the general climate. I became mired in politics. I even wrote a case study for graduate school on the organization's issues caused by Bob's leadership style and distributed it to the staff. I even gave a copy of the paper to Bob, naively thinking I could help him see the effects of his actions. I was blinded by my zeal and, in the process, cut off the hand that had fed me. I did not recognize the disconnect between the rational goals I understood to be the organization's mission and the needs of its members—especially its boss. I was preoccupied with fixing problems rather than being part of a process to help the organization heal from its rapid changes.

With a graduate degree in my hand and a smoldering bridge behind me, I hung out my shingle. At this time, my history of independence and one of my father's favorite Mozart stories helped me:

> Mozart had a student. After satisfactorily completing an assignment in compositional theory, the student asked Mozart if he should write something. Mozart suggested he write a minuet (a short piece of music for piano). The student became incensed and reminded Mozart that he had written a symphony before he was even a teenager, to which Mozart replied, "Ah, yes, but I never asked anyone."

Mozart's reply is my mantra for work. It came in handy after graduate school and leaving my position as director of research. I had a vision of entering the world of consulting, but interviews with many of the top firms changed my mind. It just didn't feel right. While I figured out what I wanted to do, I worked as a temp. I knew that the best paying jobs were for people with specific computer skills. Having never used presentation software but utterly confident of my abilities to figure out any piece of software, I consented to audition my unknown skills. Mozart did not fail me then, or any of the other dozens of times I have heeded his sage counsel.

Work has never been real, and it never has been anything more than a natural extension of my life. When I started my independent consultancy, Personal Coaching and Consulting, and it evolved it into a full-fledged business, it was always play. Even failures were like smoking beakers with mysterious chemical compounds waiting for me to discover their secrets. I could hear Great-grandpa Moschella coaxing me to turn them into lemonades. One very expensive failure resulted in the publication of my first book. There were twists and turns every step of the way. Work is like a grand boxing match where only the best bobbers and weavers stand a chance to dodge the flurry of punches, only to face another set.

This is not to say work is always fun and games. As a consultant it was painful to walk into organizations and see all of the ways we make work miserable. For example, while working for a major defense contractor, I was tasked with improving the communication skills of middle-level managers and line employees in a plant that was going to be shut down. Unfortunately, I did not have the option of declining the gig. This was a tall order given senior management's penchant for lying. Many of the people in my workshops were going to be laid off. Tensions were high. I was not inclined to paint a rosy picture, but I had to find a way to give these people something to hang on to. It turned out that openness, honesty, and the opportunities to develop relationships with one another gave these people shared strength and cause for hope.

Somehow I thought I would never be a victim of the draining exigencies experienced by these employees. I should have known better than to assume immunity. After getting married I decided to curtail my travel and take a full-time position. After the first month I was pulling my hair out. Not only was I confined physically to a cubical, but I felt that my talents were kept under lock and key. My time was wasted. Despite my efforts to take initiative and start new projects, this company ignored my energies. I was assigned to punch the clock, eat the snacks provided to me, and shut up. After three rounds of layoffs and eight months of spinning my wheels, I took a severance package and regained my freedom. During this time, I was one of many people debilitated by a negative environment. I fought off the uncertainty of the future, but I was huddled around the water cooler along with my colleagues wondering whose number was going to be called next. We were capsized by fear.

I try never to look back. There is no time to harbor bitterness. My past informs the present and fuels my dreams of the future. I need to think in motion, and the nature of my work demands that I recreate myself each moment. Although it has barely been 18 months, the best position I have ever held has been father, and the second best position I've held is son. One ties the other together and offers each of us new possibilities.

I hope that your world of work will be different. I can offer you hope, but you must be your own dreamer. Sail on your dreams and the dreams of others. So much is possible when we share our passions.

Work should be a dance. I have learned that whatever I do I can only be as good as what I can create in the moment. Be sure to appreciate others' talents. Celebrate their successes. There are no enemies, just people with different values and ideas. Avoid the people who might want to hurt you, but these are few and far between. Mostly there are great divides between ourselves and others due to our differences and our inability to extend our boundary of self to include someone else's needs and fears. The people who challenge you are your greatest learning allies. A little pain can go a long way in expanding your horizons. Work becomes arduous if we are pulled into the trap of needing to prove ourselves. No one needs proof; only we do—and that is best found in how we creatively attend to actualizing our talents. Tomorrow is no better than today, and circumstances may change 180 degrees—so be agile. Being settled means being prepared to anticipate the next creative moment.

Analysis of Sample Collage #1

This story collage helped me gather my key stories about work. The collage acted as a focusing device. I used the story collage to understand my relationship to work. Finding my stories helped me reflect on the values and meaning of work

Mother Sea

Scuba diving in the kelp beds

On the beach as a little boy

Pursuing an Abalone Shell

Fish Breathing Under Water

Fragile	Power	Abandonment	Life	Pursuit
Vulnerable	Invitation	Joy	Breath	Control
Waves		Floating	Air	Hunter
Beach		Soaring	Oxygen	Dominion
Drowning		Freedom	Connection	
			Partnership	

in my life. I decided to weave these stories together in the form of a letter. None of the stories are long. They are meant to be a tapestry. Any combination of these stories can be used in different settings. For example, in a conversation with someone I might select fewer stories but share them in greater detail. The act of physically creating the story collage creates a strong index. Putting stories to work requires us to be more purposeful and mindful of our stories and their interrelationships. Story Collaging is an excellent technique for becoming more conscious of our stories so they are readily available to us when we need them.

Sample Collage #2: Reflections on the Sea

White, frothing foam spews from her mouth. Her formless hands wrap around the ankles of an unsuspecting child. He is busy savoring his bliss on the sandy shore. Joy and disaster duel. Mother Sea bides her directives, but she will not be governed. She is content with the struggle. Her maternal instinct directs a drama that teeters on a precarious precipice between diametrically opposed outcomes. There is a tumble. Balance gives way to terror, and abandonment dominates the scene. In rushes the hero. She whisks the child from Mother Sea's loving arms. An instant passes, impinging a memory forever. It is business as usual. Ebbs and flows, nothing more.

That was my first encounter with the Pacific Ocean. Years pass, and boyhood fears give way to insatiable curiosities.

Now I am kneeling on the bottom, fully equipped with my arsenal of life-sustaining paraphernalia. Maybe it is some unconscious longing to return to the weightless fetus of my beginnings. Somehow it is right. My bubbles rise to the surface, expanding throughout their journey, and arrive as shouts of joy. I am a guest.

Today my hostess gives me a special treat. A forest of kelp weaves canopies over me. The sun aims its beams through any opening it can find. As it is above, so it is below. I am transfixed. The clatter of daily life disappears and the cold water baptizes me anew. I am adrift in a watery reverie mesmerized by the balladic ease of my fluid movements. A fish docked alongside the kelp catches my eye. My arms flow toward it, and, as they make their way through the viscous medium, I swear I can feel its pulsing gills vibrating through the water. It is as if I am tethered to the fish. Its gill and my finger are joined in some magnetic union. I am struck by the obvious. This fish does not know it is in water. The water is air to the fish. Yet I experience the water as some sort of cosmic glue tying me, and everything around me in a synergistic partnership. The fish knows none of this.

The arrow of time moves forward, and the scene changes again. This time I am cutting through the water in pursuit of adventure. The hunter-gatherer instinct inside me stirs and my eye is caught by the scintillating glimmer of an abalone shell tucked in a tight crib of rocks. Priding myself on my acrobatic agility, I position myself just right to reach in and take Mother Sea's treasure. Disorientation ensues, and a mouthful of water assaults me. Several efforts of gear and dive buddy offer no remedy to my situation. I must make the climb to the surface without air. Perhaps this is the freedom I have longed for with Mother Sea all along.

I am caught between worlds—one of land and one of water. To which of the two do I belong? Each is a part of my nature, yet neither fully meets my needs. I need them both, and they need me.

We are made mostly of water. Toss in a few atoms of carbon and other trace minerals, let evolution work a trick or two, and we emerge. There must be some sort of galactic museum. "Planet Earth exhibit this way," the sign reads. The centerpiece of the exhibit is a stuffed Homo sapiens. Maybe the caption reads, "big on brains, short on awareness—a highly differentiated life form with a lack of integration between itself and its environment."

Could we be a natural wonder of the universe? Maybe it is we who should invoke the celestial muses and tune ourselves to the frequency of wonder.

There is more water than land. We can reach higher into the heavens than we can into the belly of our home. We fear the deep. Is it the thought of a colossal squid or is it an avoidance of our nature?

Nature is in flux. A fire is constructive. Fertilizer is destructive. All natural ingredients include synthesized chemicals as part of the standard du jour menu. Call in the relativists. They will save us. Nurture not nature is to blame. Social constructs are the root of all evils. I forgot, could you tell me who built the constructs? Or maybe it's all predetermined in our genes. Just fill out this form and the human genome is yours for analysis. I can see street-corner hawkers vying for our attention, "Hear ye, hear ye, get your DVD today, and read all about your genetic makeup."

I put up the mirror and spin around. Give me somewhere to point my finger. There must be a cause to hang my hat on today. Resources are not finite; only our understanding of how to manage and control them is lacking, is it not?

The fish turns to me. Its beady stare shifts my attention.

I reach out to touch it but I realize the fish is inside me. It is a part of my memory—a vital epiphany guiding me. It slips through my fingers, and the momentary gift is lost. I am back to the ranting ramblings of my mind.

The equilibrium is gone. I throw off the cover of the hot tub and subject the water to my tests. If I have read my instruments correctly, I can bring this water back to a happy, safe balance. The water will succumb to my elixir. I do not need to banish my ideal. I am master of the water.

A mother holds her child's hand as she leads him to the great expanse of the sea for the first time. Eyes filled with awe, he lets go of her hand. He takes all of it in and only some of it registers. Mother Sea will take hold of his imagination in ways beyond his present capacity of comprehension, even if she must pull him toward her bosom.

Our event horizon must stretch further than our puny minds allow us. Nature goes about its business. One thing is obliterated and replaced by another. A phoenix rises out of the ashes to take flight once again. What about those mighty dinosaurs or species of plants and insects off our radar screens that are candles blown out in the dark before anyone benefits from their illuminating secrets? Nature has not gone astray; it is simply in motion.

I examine my hand. I am appalled to realize that every seven years almost all the cells in my body are replaced. Those poor cells remind me of pelagic carcasses unknowingly com-

mitted to insane asylums of our shores. Have I lost my nature or am I along for the ride? Maybe I should just catch a wave and sit on top of the world.

I hold the treasure in my hand. The pearly allure of the abalone's shell is intoxicating my thoughts. I am without air but I am free. Whatever happened to my umbilical cord? I will break to the surface and rejoin the atmosphere. The fabric of water will be punctuated with my staccato gasps for air underscored by my drive to be unique and in control. I want to bring the fish to the surface. Will it feel the air as joining the two of us in a new dance, or will the harsh reality of a foreign environment take hold of it before it is enlightened?

The world marches to its own nature. Developing nations are eager to karaoke tunes they have heard before, and scarce resources attempt counterpoint melodies against the beat of progress. Mother Sea beckons, a child is initiated, and an underwater explorer struggles against his nature to hold on to his battling prizes of material gain and insight. There is a faint glimmer of guidance. Mother Sea scans the shore and finds another child eager for tutelage. Perhaps her passion to incite wonder might take hold and pique a new imagination.

Analysis of Sample Collage #2

I was asked to write a thought-provoking essay about the sea. This example contains fewer stories, but reflecting on the three central stories in the piece ushered in many feelings and images. Stories became the poetry of my mind. The stories were the backdrop on which I projected my imagination of the sea. When we start working with our stories in relation to one another, we find ourselves in a sea of reverie and insights. They start looking less one-dimensional and more three-dimensional. The themes from the stories start morphing into and out of one another. We realize that stories are onions with layers and layers of meaning. We are able to discern the layers of our stories by using other stories to understand them. Although this may sound fantastical, the mind opens up to a whole new set of possibilities. Our perception of the world, and of others, is fundamentally altered.

The two examples of story collages emphasize some of the personal ways story collages can be used. However, story collages also work well with groups. I have used story collages with project teams to conduct after-action reviews. In such cases, individuals capture their experiences of working on the project. The facilitator's task is to help people see the connections between people, stories, and key lessons learned, and then use the stories as a springboard to help people move past unresolved feelings and imagine how to build upon the successes and failures of the project at hand. I have used story collages to help organizations understand their internal and external customers. I have used story collages in arbitration, negotiations, strategic planning, user requirements meetings, and product development sessions. The possibilities are limitless. The best results will be achieved

when people are accustomed to working with their stories, so I suggest doing some prep work with people to develop their story competencies. For more ideas and exercises on how to develop your communication competencies through stories, see my book, *The Strategic Use of Stories in Organizational Communication and Learning.*

SUMMARY

Putting stories to work requires a good index. Stories are more powerful when they are pieced together than when they are used in isolation. Story collages are a tool for building an index and discovering the interrelationships between stories.

9 / *Exercises and Tools*

THIS CHAPTER CONTAINS exercises to practice putting stories to work. The first section lists guidelines and identifies practice opportunities on how to develop keener observational skills in organizations through stories. The second section describes nine exercises that can be used in any type of workshop or meeting to help participants develop stronger story skills.

OBSERVATIONAL SKILLS

Awareness of our stories and the interconnections between them gives us freedom to behave in new ways. We are not complete slaves to our reactive tendencies. Carl Jung uses an example of three people preparing to cross a stream to illustrate the nature of human behavior. Because the stream is wide, it is not possible to jump across it. Each person approaches the stream differently. One person looks at the stream and impulsively decides to jump across it and take his or her chances on getting wet. The other person decides not to chance it and walks along the stream looking for a good place to cross. The third person searches for a log to place across the stream so that he or she can cross it.

Each of us can identify with one of the characters in the story. I know what I would do. My first instinct would be an impulsive one. I would try to jump across the stream and hope I didn't get wet; if I did get wet, I wouldn't let it bother me too much.

There's a paradox here. On the one hand, we have an identity that prescribes many of our thoughts, emotions, perceptions, and behaviors; but, on the other hand, we are also free to choose how we will act. Each of us has a preferred behavior that is somehow tied to our identity. For the moment, let's forget the classical debate of nature versus nurture. I think it's reasonable to assume that we are defined by some combination of the two. Aspects of our identities are encoded in our genetics and our experiences—to what degree and how is not of concern right now. Therefore, who and how we are is not completely hard-wired.

Our experiences are transformed into memories that are encoded in our minds as stories. Although we have a relatively stable identity (evidenced by our consistent words, attitudes, beliefs, and behaviors), we are also capable of changing. Being aware of our identities and predispositions allows us the possibility of acting differently. We are not locked into one story. Despite my impulse to jump across the stream, I am also free to search for a better place to cross it or to find a log.

If I am aware of my guiding stories, I will grant myself the possibility to bypass my default behavior and act in a novel way. As discussed earlier in the book, if I am aware of my story, I am not bound by it, and I can adopt different ones. This does not mean that every time I come to the stream, I will not jump impulsively across it. What it does mean is that each time I come to the stream, I am free to consider my actions and imagine alternative ones. We are capable of being far more fluid and dynamic in our thoughts and behavior than conventional wisdom dictates. I wish to reemphasize the word "possibility." I am not denying the existence of identity and character traits. I am simply pointing out that there is a relationship between stories, self-awareness, and behavior.

The relationship between stories and behavior is an indirect one but central to our discussion of the role stories play in business. The picture in Figure 9.1 of an iceberg summarizes the various levels on which stories operate.

Levels of the Iceberg

Telling

We share stories as a principal way of communicating. When someone tells a story, we usually respond with a story of our own, and even if we don't, we recall one in our mind to understand what that person is saying. Having many stories to tell makes us versatile communicators.

Learning

We use stories to transmit learning. If a picture is worth a thousand words, a story is worth a thousand pictures. Complex and intricate thoughts and ideas can be elegantly encoded in stories.

Stories map to one another. We create relationships between stories and look for parallels between them. In this way, stories are building blocks for learning. We

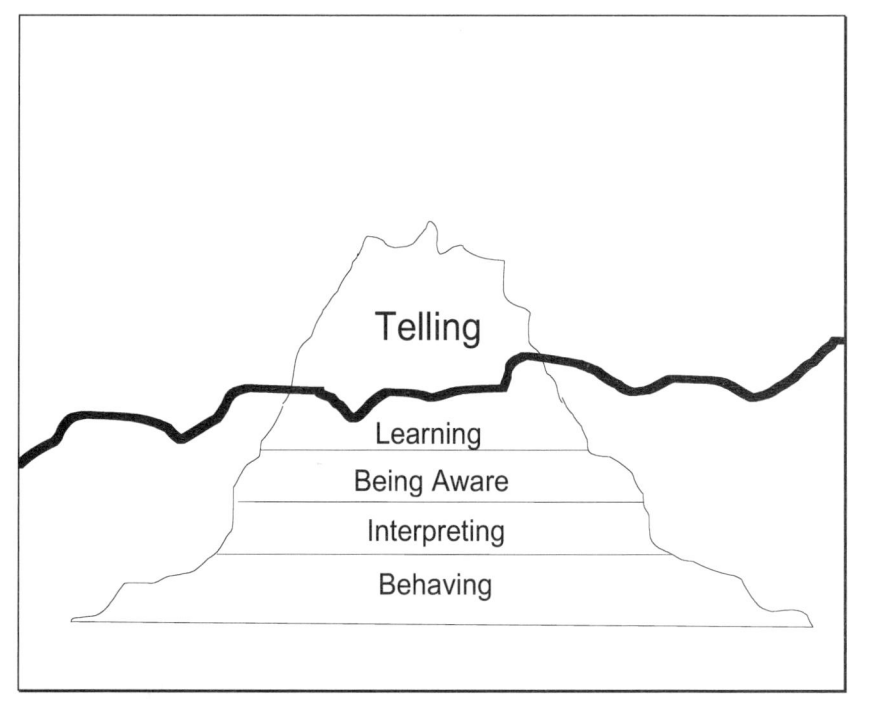

Figure 9.1

learn by associating new pieces of information with existing information. When experience remains isolated in a single domain, it is horribly inefficient. Recall Roger Schank's definition of intelligence from chapter 8, which asserts that intelligence is the ability to easily index our vast array of experiences and make connections between old ones and new ones.

Being Aware

Because our experiences play a large role in forming who we are, stories are used to gain self-awareness. Our stories contain vital clues to who we are and how we view the world. We need to reflect on our experiences to get the most out of them.

Stories are like watching a videotape of our experiences. They give us access to our memories and provide a medium through which we can analyze the impact of these memories on our perceptions and identities.

Interpreting

We are constantly crafting stories to explain the world. However, it's important to realize that our interpretations are filtered through our perceptions, beliefs, attitudes, and biases.

The stories we craft are theories. We develop our "story theory" by combining our observations with perceptual filters. Our perceptual filters develop over time as a result of our experiences. And our experiences are accessible to us through memories that are archived in our minds as stories.

Behaving

We use stories to explain behavior and develop strategies for how to interact with other people.

We are also capable of considering alternative behaviors that go against our ingrained ones by being aware of stories that describe our nature and by imagining different ones.

Stories are the templates onto which new behaviors can be projected and through which they can be actualized. We use stories to gain an understanding of who we are. Collectively our stories paint an accurate picture of who we are. If we can access this information, we give ourselves freedom. In other words, we can break out of an old story and temporarily adopt a new one.

Each layer is built upon the previous one. Learning through stories cannot occur if we do not have a vast index of stories to draw from. We cannot be aware of how our stories affect us if we do not use stories as a vehicle for learning. A key component of learning entails observing the world around us and interpreting what we see. If we are not aware of how we have formed many of our perceptual filters, then we will not know how we have come to our current theory. And if we are not conscious of what story we are creating to interpret our observations, we will not be able to choose our actions.

OBSERVATION EXERCISES

This section contains exercises to guide observation of your business environment. The exercises suggest things to look for in certain situations. You will use all the information gathered from your observations to draw preliminary theories and conclusions. Once you are more aware of some of your perceptual filters, having gone through all the personal reflections from the previous chapter, you can craft stories to explain your observations. Use these stories to guide your behavior and plan your actions, as opposed to simply reacting to people and situations.

The topics with regard to business observations include:

1. First impressions
2. Office decorations
3. Telephone calls
4. Meetings

5. Sales presentations
6. Customer interactions
7. Corporate culture
8. The day in review

This is by no means an exhaustive list. You can add your own observation topics to the list, but this should be a good starting point.

These topics do not need to be approached in any particular order, and they can be used in a variety of ways. These observations can be made all the time. Until it becomes second nature, use the following two tables to get started. Table 9.1 will help guide your observations, and Table 9.2 will help you record your observations and story interpretations.

Use the first column in Table 9.1—*Things to Observe*—to record some ideas of things to pay attention to, to get you going. Use the second column—*Questions*—to record some questions intended to direct your attention to specific things. You should try to answer as many of these questions as possible.

Table 9.1

Things to Observe	Questions

Use the first column of Table 9.2—*Actual Observations*—to record a brief description of what you observe. Use the second column—*Plausible Story*—to record your interpretation of the observations. In other words, what sort of conclusions can you draw or postulate based upon your observations? Use the third column—*Implications*—to indicate how the conclusions you have drawn have been affected by other stories, especially personal ones and your perceptual filters. Then decide which story will guide your behavior.

Table 9.2

Actual Observations	Plausible Story	Implications

Let's go through an example. The business context/topic for this example will be "first impressions" during an interview of a potential employee. The example will be limited to one set of observations.

In the first column I record my observations. Taking note of these observations helps me realize what is catching my attention. Next I need to interpret my observations. I want to explain what I am observing. I piece together my observations to form a story. My perceptual filters and personal history affect the story I generate to explain what I am observing about the candidate. Remember the example from the previous chapter about how hard my sister and I worked and the sacrifices we made for our education? Because of my personal history, I have a bias against this candidate. I am unlikely to hire the candidate even though he or she may be the right person for the job.

Instead of passively allowing my story to dictate my behavior of not wanting to hire the candidate, I decide that the best course of action will be to let another person hold another interview.

Table 9.3

Actual Observation	Plausible Story	Implications
Candidate is young and appears eager to impress me. Candidate has very little work experience. Candidate describes himself as a fast learner because he never had to study hard to get good grades. Candidate makes a gloating remark about never having to make money by doing "menial jobs." Candidate grew up in an affluent area. Candidate keeps emphasizing how hard he plans to work at the company. Candidate believes he can rise quickly in the company. Candidate has no brothers or sisters.	As an only child from a wealthy family, this person has been fortunate to receive an excellent education. He has never had to work hard and seems proud of that. However, he keeps emphasizing how hard he plans to work at the company, which, given the circumstances, does not seem believable. Although the candidate is very confident and articulate, he is not a good match for the job.	I worked my way through high school and college washing dishes and answering switchboards. Kids who get everything handed to them on a silver platter do not know the value of working hard. I need to find out more about this candidate and ask another person who is not biased in the same ways to interview him before dismissing him as a candidate.

Business Observations Topic 1: First Impressions

We form impressions of people very quickly, and first impressions can have a lasting impact on our opinion of a person. Here are some things to be aware of when you are meeting someone for the first time.

Things to Observe	Questions
Clothing	Is it appropriate?
	How would you characterize his clothing?
	Is she well groomed?
Eye contact	Does he make good eye contact?
	Do her eyes dart about?
	Is he nervous?
	Does she seem distracted?
	Is he interested in you?
Handshake	Is it firm? Limp? Vigorous? Warm? Cold?
	Is it short in duration?
	Is it long in duration?
Posture	Does she stand tall?
	Is he stiff?
	Does she slouch?
	Is his chin forward? Up?
	How close is she standing to you?
	Do you notice any injuries or physical impairments?
Conversation	Does he ask questions?
	What does she like talking about?
	How would you characterize his voice?
	Does she gesticulate a lot?
	Does he have speech patterns?
	Does she use any words or phrases a lot?
	What filter words or crutch words does he use?
Facial expressions	Does she laugh a lot?
	Does he smile?
	Does she raise her eyebrows?
	Does his forehead wrinkle when he speaks?

Business Observations Topic 2: Office Decorations

It's always fun to walk into offices and see how people have decorated them. Decorations can quickly tell you a lot about what is important and meaningful to a person.

Things to Observe	Questions
Pictures	Does he have pictures of his spouse or significant other?
	Does she have pictures of her parents?

	Does he have pictures of his children?
	Does she have pictures of herself?
	Are there pictures of special occasions?
	Are there pictures of him on vacation?
	Are there pictures of her involved in hobbies or sports?
Diplomas and awards	What diplomas and awards are displayed in the office?
Decorations	Are there any sayings or mottos displayed?
	Does he have plants?
	Does she have any toys?
	What knickknacks are there?
	What posters does he have?
	What type of screensaver does she have?
	Does he put up holiday decorations?
	What type of calendar does she have?
	What kind of music does he listen to?
Organization	Is the office neat or messy?
	How is the furniture arranged?
	Does she appear to be working on many things at the same time?

Business Observations Topic 3: Telephone Calls

Many people spend a lot of time at work on the telephone. We can tell much about a person's communication style and temperament by how he or she speaks on the phone.

Things to Observe	Questions
Answering the phone	Is he polite? Rude?
	Is she impatient?
	Does he answer with a formal greeting or a standard "hello"?
	If she has caller ID, does she greet the caller by name?
	How does his tone of voice change in response to the caller?
	Does she use a speaker phone?
Conversations	Is he doing anything else while he's on the phone?
	Is she long winded?

	Can you tell whether he is listening to the caller?
	How would you characterize her rapport with the caller?
	Can you tell whether anyone is controlling the conversation?
	Does his facial expression match his tone and voice?
	What is the nature of the call?
	How does she interact with customer service representatives?
	How does he treat his wife on the phone?
	Family? Children? Friends?
Ending a call	Can you tell whether it was a productive call?
	Does she make excuses to get off the phone?
	Does the call end on a personal note?

Business Observations Topic 4: Meetings

Meetings are an excellent time to assess valuable information about people and organizational dynamics and rework our stories.

Things to Observe	Questions
Meeting mechanics	Who is attending, and what are their roles?
	Who is leading the meeting?
	Is there an agenda?
	Are food and beverages provided?
	Where are people sitting?
	Is it an informational meeting? Decision making? Both?
	Did the meeting start on time?
	Did the meeting stay within its designated time period?
	Did anyone leave unexpectedly or take phone calls during the meeting?
Interpersonal dynamics	Did people come prepared to the meeting?
	Who is dominating the meeting?
	Do people appear to be comfortable expressing their views and opinions?
	Are there key issues not being discussed?
	Do there appear to be alliances in the room?

	How would you characterize people's body language?
	What key things were said during the meeting?
	Is anyone acting aloof or indifferent?
	Is anyone distorting information?
Outcomes	Did anyone leave the meeting upset?
	What aspects of the meeting went well?
	What aspects of the meeting went poorly?
	Was everything on the agenda covered?
	What are the action items?
	Do people follow through on their action items?

Business Observations Topic 5: Sales Presentations

How your company presents itself to customers is key to its success. It is necessary to constantly gauge customers' perceptions and needs. Observing sales presentations is a great way to do this. The information gathered will help your company continually revise its sales and marketing strategy by adopting new stories.

Things to Observe	Questions
Setting	Who is the audience?
	Where is the presentation being made?
	How many people are attending, and what are their roles?
	What is the customer's expectation of the presentation?
Delivery	Is it a canned presentation?
	Did the presenter assess what the customer already knows about the product?
	How did the presenter involve the customer in the presentation?
	How much does the presenter know about the company?
	Does the presenter use examples and explanations relevant to the customer?
	How much do you learn about the customer during the presentation?
	What sort of rapport does the presenter develop with the customer?

Customer reactions	During the presentation what body language do the participants exhibit?
	What questions do the customers ask?
	What caught the customers' attention?
	What concerns do the customers have about the product or service?

Business Observations Topic 6: Customer Interactions

Watching or listening to customer service representatives interact with customers reveals a great deal about their people skills. In addition, observations of customer interactions enable accurate assessment of the company's customer service business processes and customers' needs.

Things to Observe	Questions
Customer	What is the customer's issue?
	How does the customer articulate the issue?
	What is her tone of voice?
	What is his body language?
	Does the customer perceive that he or she has been heard and understood?
Customer service representative	How does she greet the customer?
	What is his tone of voice?
	What is her body language?
	Is he listening?
	What questions does she ask to understand the customer's needs?
	Does he understand the customer's need?
	Is she able to defuse a tense situation?
	Does he become defensive?
Actions and resolutions	What steps are taken to resolve the customer's issue?
	What does the customer expect?
	Are there any policies or business processes limiting the actions of the customer service representative?
	Does the customer service representative have access to all the information he or she needs?
	Does the customer service representative offer alternatives?
	How could this customer interaction have been handled differently?

Is the customer satisfied?

How does the customer service representative feel?

Business Observations Topic 7: Corporate Culture

For any organization, corporate culture is elusive and difficult to define. However, some observations of the environment can shed light on a company's culture.

Things to Observe	Questions
Office dynamics	Who are the people who wield the most power in the organization?
	How did they acquire this power?
	Who eats lunch with whom?
	Are there cliques?
	Do people gossip? About what?
	With whom are some of the key leaders aligned within the organization?
	Do people trust one another?
	Do people help one another?
	Do people work as a team?
Sacred cows	Are there any people who are above reproach in the organization?
	Are there any business practices or processes that cannot be challenged?
	Are there any company policies that will never change?
	What are the most cherished values, beliefs, and ideals of the organization?
Legends and myths	Who are the heroes in the organization?
	How did the organization become successful and grow?
	What stories do people like to tell about the organization?
Rallying points	What benefits does the organization offer its employees?
	What in the organization are people proud of?
	How are people motivated?
	How are people recognized and rewarded for their contributions?

Business Observations Topic 8: The Day in Review

Getting into the habit of taking a few moments at the end of every day to recall the day's events will help you gain insights. Try to visualize the people you interacted with, the things you said to them, the things they said to you, the actions you took, and the actions you wanted to take but failed to do so.

Things to Observe	Questions
Conversations	Whom did you speak with today?
	What did they want from you?
	What did you want from them?
	Did you get what you needed? If not, why?
	How did your mood affect your interactions with others?
	Were there any personal matters on your mind?
	Were you insensitive to anyone's feelings?
	Did you say anything you did not want to?
	Did anyone say anything that upset you?
	Did you recognize anyone's contribution?
	What compliments did you receive?
Actions taken	Did you forget to do anything?
	What did you need to accomplish today?
	What did you accomplish?
	Did you hit your targets? If no, why not?
	Did you need to rearrange any of your priorities?
	What's the most notable thing that happened?
	How did you help other people?
	Did you hinder anyone else's work?
	What effect did you have on others?
	How did other people's actions affect you?
	If you could undo any actions taken, what would they be?

EXERCISES TO DEVELOP STORY SKILLS

These are some of my favorite workshop exercises. They are flexible and can be used to accomplish a variety of objectives. I have used them to teach specific story skills in "story workshops," and I have also used them in more general ways. For the most part they are simple to lead but can have some profound effects. Here is a summary of the exercises:

Exercises	Objectives
1. Tell me who you are	Experience storytelling as a more active and effective way of communicating. Build rapport between people. Enable participants to discover that they have a wealth of stories. Discover the difference between didactic forms of communication and storytelling.
2. Family story	Practice telling stories. Practice listening to stories. Learn storytelling techniques. Identify what makes one story more interesting than another. Encounter the role of vulnerability in stories.
3. The story of the man who had no stories	Explore how stories work. Practice analyzing a story. Discover how stories encode information.
4. Story prompts	Illustrate how stories can be triggered. Practice looking for connections and relationships.
5. Grab bag	Illustrate how stories can be triggered. Work with random objects to remember stories. Practice looking for connections and relationships.
6. Clichés	Find a story to illustrate a cliché. Use stories to visualize abstractions. Practice thinking in stories. Practice telling stories.
7. Capture and recapture	Record a memory and see how others reconstruct it. Understand the relationships between memories, perceptions, and stories.
8. Story dialogue	Become aware of how stories are part of communicating. Conduct a conversation with only stories.
9. Joanna Macy's learning to see each other	Learn to shift your perspective to compassionately encounter another person. Demonstrate the role of empathy in stories. Imagine another person's perspective.

Exercise 1: Tell Me Who You Are (50–60 Minutes)

Instructions

1. Have people pair off, if possible with someone they do not know.
2. Instruct one person to talk about himself or herself while the other listens. The listener cannot speak or ask any questions.
3. After 10 to 15 minutes, have them switch roles.
4. Debrief the exercise.

Facilitating

This is an interesting exercise to watch. At first, many people dislike or are uncomfortable talking about themselves. They feel that they have very little to say, and that their lives are not very interesting. Typically, people approach the exercise like an interview. They begin rattling off the facts of their lives (e.g., where they were born, raised, went to school, and worked). Before long they run out of things to say, but there is usually a lot of time left. Without realizing what they are doing, they begin telling a story. Suddenly time begins to compress, they realize they have a lot to say, and they become more animated. A change in the listeners is also usually observed. Listeners lean forward and become more involved in what the speaker is saying.

After the exercise, ask participants to share their experiences and observations. See whether they can identify when they switched from fact-relating mode to storytelling mode. Go around the room and ask people to give examples. Encourage them to draw parallels between the exercise and communication in general. See whether people can recall similar experiences, such as when they had trouble communicating or used a story.

Exercise 2: Family Story (90–120 Minutes)

Instructions

1. Create groups of four or five people.
2. Have everyone in the group tell two or more family or childhood stories. The stories should be about the participant or about a relative, sibling, or childhood friend.
3. After listening to each story, the group selects two stories to tell to the group at large and designates a spokesperson.
4. Each group tells the stories it selected.
5. Debrief the exercises.

Variation

This exercise also works well with pairs. Ask each person to select one of the partner's stories and retell it to the group.

Facilitating

This exercise gives people experience in active listening. Retelling another person's story and bringing it alive for others is not as easy as it may seem. In order to experience a story, the imagination must be actively working. Ask participants to pay attention to how much detail they include in their retelling. Ask those recounting the stories to explain why they selected them.

Ask the original storyteller to evaluate the retelling of it. If appropriate, ask the originator to share the insights that the story reveals about him or her as a person. This often happens without having to ask. Ask the same question of the group at large. This is especially fascinating when people know each other fairly well. A word of warning that you may get more than you bargained for, because stories can be very revealing. However, they also can be used to reinforce inaccurate and self-serving perceptions. These discussions should be handled with care.

Exercise 3: The Story of the Man Who Had No Stories (90 Minutes)

Instructions

1. Tell the following story to the group.
2. After telling the story, create groups of four or five.
3. Hand out copies of the story to everyone.
4. Instruct people to read the story on their own and then discuss it with their group.
5. Give each group a flip chart. Ask the groups to analyze the story. What can they learn from it about the nature of stories?
6. Let the groups work for 30 minutes.
7. Start a large-group discussion by asking each group to report on its work.

The Story

Liam was a basket weaver. He would cut rushes, make them into baskets, and sell them in nearby towns. After some time, there were no rushes left.

He knew of a glen far away where fine rushes were reputed to grow. But it was a fairy glen and nobody dared go there. However, Liam's money had run out, and he was desperate, so he decided to take a risk. With his knife, a rope, and the lunch his wife packed for him, Liam set out for the glen.

He had cut and tied two fine bundles of rushes when a thick mist began to form around him. Thinking the fog would clear soon, he sat down and ate his lunch. By the time he had finished eating, it was so foggy he could not even see his hands.

Liam became disoriented. He stood up and looked to the east and looked to the west. He saw a light in the distance and thought, "Where there is light there's bound to be people." So he set out for the light and eventually came upon a farmhouse with the door standing open. Liam entered and found an old man and woman sitting by a fire. "Come in and get warm," they said. After exchanging some pleasantries, the old man asked Liam to tell a story.

"I can't," said Liam. "I've never told a story."

The woman turned to him and said, "Then go down to the well and bring us a bucket of water for your keep."

"I'd be happy to, as long as I don't have to tell a story," replied Liam.

Liam went down to the well and filled the bucket. He set the bucket down for a moment so the outside of it could dry before he brought it in. Suddenly, the wind roared and swept him high into the sky. It blew him to the east, and it blew him to the west. When he fell back to Earth, there was no bucket, and no well, and no farmhouse. But again, off in the distance, he saw a light and he thought, "Where there is light there's bound to be people." So he set out for the light, and after some time, he found that it came from a farmhouse far bigger than the first, with lights shining out of the door.

When he entered, Liam saw that he had come to a wake-house. There were two rows of men sitting along the back wall, and a girl with black curly hair sat by the fire. She welcomed Liam and asked him to sit beside her.

Liam had barely sat down when a big man stood up. "It's not a real wake without a fiddler. I'll go get one so that we can start dancing."

"Don't go," said the girl with black curly hair. "The best fiddler in Ireland is here." And she looked straight at Liam.

"Oh, no," said Liam. "I can't play a tune on a fiddle. I've got no music in my head."

"Sure you can," insisted the girl, and she pushed a fiddle and bow into his hands and he played away. Everyone agreed they had never heard a better fiddler than Liam.

They danced and danced until the big man said that was enough. "We must go get a priest to say Mass. This corpse must leave before daybreak."

"There's no need," said the girl with black curly hair. "The best priest in Ireland is sitting right here." And again she looked straight at Liam.

"Oh no," said Liam. "I'm no priest. I know nothing about a priest's work."

"Sure you do," she said. "You will do it just as well as you did the fiddling."

Before Liam knew it, he was standing at the altar saying Mass. And they all said that they'd never heard any priest say a better Mass than Liam.

Then the corpse was put in the coffin, and four men took it on their shoulders. Three were short and one was tall, and the coffin wobbled terribly.

"We'll have to go get a doctor to cut a piece off the legs of that big man to make him the same height as the others," said one of the men.

"Stay here," said the girl. "The best doctor in all of Ireland is here among us." And again she looked straight at Liam.

"Oh no," said Liam. "I've never done any doctoring. I couldn't possibly do it."

"Sure you can," she said.

And she thrust a scalpel into his hand. Liam cut a piece from each of the big man's legs, under his knees, and stuck the legs back on and made him the same height as the other three. Everyone marveled at Liam's doctoring skills, and all agreed they had never seen a better doctor in all of Ireland.

They picked up the coffin and walked carefully to the graveyard. There was a big stone wall around the graveyard, 10 or 12 feet high. They all climbed the wall to the graveyard on the other side. The last man on top of the wall was Liam.

At that moment, a big blast of wind swept him into the sky. It blew him to the east, and it blew him to the west. When he fell back to Earth there was no graveyard, or wall, or coffin, or funeral. He had fallen by the well where he had gone to fetch some water. The water had not even dried off the bucket.

Liam took the bucket into the house. The old man and woman were there just as he had left them. He put the bucket down beside them.

"Now, Liam," said the old man, "can you tell us a story?"

"I can," said he. "I am a man with a story to tell." And he told them about everything that had happened to him.

"Well, Liam," said the old man, "from now on, if anybody asks you to tell a story, tell them that story; you are a man who has a story to tell."

They gave him a bed, and Liam fell asleep, for he was tired after all he had gone through.

When he woke in the morning, he was lying in the fairy glen with his head on the two bundles of rushes. He got up and went home and he never worked another day in his life.

Facilitating

Practice telling the story. It is important that you are comfortable with the story. It may be helpful to reread the first part of the book to review the different ways stories can function.

This story always generates a rich discussion. If groups get stuck on their analyses of the story, offer some ideas on what a story is and how and why a story works. Then turn their attention back to the text.

Exercise 4: Story Prompts (60–90 Minutes)

Instructions

1. Draw two columns on a flip chart or board and label them Roles and Actions.

Roles	Actions

2. Instruct participants to think about the various roles they play at work and at home and write them down in the Roles column.
3. Create a list of things they do in the Actions column. Help by suggesting that one way of generating a list is to think about what actions they perform in the roles they listed.
4. Give some examples, and then let the group work on its own for about 20 minutes.
5. Take a role from the left column and match it randomly with an action in the right column. Demonstrate with a few examples how to use the list of roles and actions to trigger stories. Give the group five minutes to look at the list and trigger stories.
6. Go around the room and ask people to share a story or two and mark on the chart the roles and actions they used to trigger the story.

Facilitating

Be sure to provide plenty of examples. I try to avoid examples I have used with other groups, because I want my stories and the triggers that aroused them to be fresh and spontaneous each time I facilitate this exercise. Seeing triggers in action will have the greatest impact on participants.

As you begin paying more attention to stories, triggering them becomes easier. We each have some sort of mental schema that indexes stories. This exercise lets people experience how to access and stimulate their indexes. Participants discover how to see interrelationships between ostensibly disconnected roles and actions.

Be supportive of those who find this exercise difficult. If necessary, randomly select an action and role for them. Others may be very clever. Push them to dig deeper.

Exercise 5: Grab Bag (3–5 Minutes per Person)

Instructions

1. Fill a bag with random objects.
2. Have each person pull an object from the bag.
3. Go around the room and ask people use the object to trigger a story.
4. Be sure to include yourself in the exercise.

Facilitation

I love a story my father-in-law told me. Sam works as a funeral director. He and his colleagues routinely challenged a certain rabbi. Before a funeral service they would give the rabbi a random word—for example, "ice cream." The rabbi had to find a way of incorporating this word into his eulogy. Without fail and to the utter amazement of Sam and his colleagues, no matter what the word was, the rabbi managed to find a connection between the word and the person he was speaking about.

Similarly, this exercise challenges participants to generate a story from a random object. This can be a nice way to wrap up a day's activities, or to reenergize a group after a difficult or draining exercise.

Encourage people to think beyond the creative aspects of cleverly fashioning a story from a random object. You want them to extend the idea of interconnectedness beyond random objects and stories. They should see that one experience or story is an opportunity to trigger another one and gain new insights. According to Roger Schank, one of the hallmarks of intelligence is the capacity to apply stories from one domain to another.

Exercise 6: Clichés (3–5 Minutes per Person)

Instructions

1. Write out some of your favorite clichés or aphorisms on index cards. Here are a few to get you started:

   "Don't cut off your nose to spite your face."

   "If life gives you lemons, make lemonade."

   "If at first you don't succeed, try, try, again."

   "At the drop of a hat."

   "You can't judge a book by its cover."

   "A stitch in time saves nine."

   "Live for today."

   "You can't see the forest for the trees."

   "It's water under the bridge."

   "What you see is what you get."

   "What's here today is gone tomorrow."

2. Ask each participant to pick an index card at random.
3. Go around the room and have people tell a story triggered by the cliché on their card.

Facilitation

This exercise gives participants confidence in triggering, indexing, and crafting stories quickly. Clichés are abstract and are criticized as overused phrases that lack specificity. Participants will see how stories bring abstractions to life. How does the story they tell connect to the cliché? Instead of articulating an idea abstractly, how quickly can they find an appropriate story to express their ideas? Help the group imagine how replacing an abstraction with a story will enable them to communicate more clearly.

Exercise 7: Capture and Recapture (60 Minutes)

Instructions

1. At the end of the day, instruct everyone to write on an index card something that happened or something that was said during the session that really stands out in his or her mind.
2. The next day, ask each participant to randomly select an index card.
3. Ask the participant to recount the event or the things that were said that led to the event or comment on the index card.
4. Compare the participant's recounting and interpretation of the event's significance with that of the person who wrote the card and with the perceptions of the rest of the group.

Facilitation

This is not an easy exercise to facilitate, and it may take a few attempts before it goes smoothly. The problem is, not every index card will yield a vigorous discussion. It is helpful to read all the cards first and select the more interesting or potentially provocative ones.

If a particular index card is not generating discussion, quickly move on to another one. Carefully choose the person who goes first. It should be someone who you are confident can reconstruct the previous day's event or comment. However, if that person is unable to tell a story, that is an important insight in and of itself. What is memorable to one person may not be important or have even registered to another.

After one person attempts to give his or her account, ask the author of the index card to share his or her recollection. How do the two accounts differ? Next, ask the group at large to share its memories and perceptions. Are there more differences?

This exercise demonstrates the role of perception. Try to help participants discover how stories are a powerful way of understanding our perceptions and the perceptions of others.

Exercise 8: Story Dialogue (60 Minutes)

Instructions

1. Ask people to pair up with a partner.
2. Give each pair a list of conversational topics. Create a list of topics for participants to choose from. Here are a few ideas:

    School and teachers

    Holidays

    Summer vacations

    Travel

    Food

    Children

3. The topics can be about anything. They can be generic like those mentioned, or they can be more specific to the people and situation. In some circumstances, I ask the pairs to come up with their own topics.
4. One person in the pair begins a conversation by telling a story. Each partner must respond to a story with a story.
5. Each person should take notes about the conversation. This only needs to be a word or two that will recall the conversation's development and progression.
6. Allow 15 minutes for the story conversations.
7. Go around the room and ask each pair to take turns describing their conversations.

Facilitation

This exercise helps people to see the role stories can play in conversation. The best response to a story is another story. However, be sure to emphasize that storytelling is not about outdoing each other with wilder and wilder tales. Rather, stories generate opportunities for defining common ground and understanding each other's experiences.

Ask the pairs to share the twists and turns of their conversation. Their notes will help. Ask participants to reflect on how their partner's stories triggered other stories. Inquire how all of the stories interrelate.

Ask the group to characterize the overall effect of stories. Do they perceive any difference between an average conversation and one from a story? Can they imagine using stories in their daily conversations? If someone can offer an example of a recent conversation, ask how would that conversation would have been different if stories had been used.

Exercise 9: Joanna Macy's Learning to See Each Other (45 Minutes)[1]

Instructions

1. Have people pair up and face their partners.
2. Explain the exercise. You will be reading a meditation written by Joanna Macy. During the meditation, each person will sit across from his or her partner and stare into the partner's eyes. At times it may be uncomfortable. We are not accustomed to holding another person's gaze for very long. Encourage people to relax and focus on the words of the meditation.
3. Read the meditation in a slow and gentle voice.
4. Discuss the meditation.

The Meditation

Take a couple of deep breaths, centering yourself and exhaling tension.... Look into each other's eyes.... If you feel discomfort or an urge to laugh or look away, just note that embarrassment with patience and gentleness, and come back, when you can, to your partner's eyes. You may never see this person again: the opportunity to behold the uniqueness of this particular human being is given to you now....

As you look into this person's eyes, let yourself become aware of the powers that are there.... Open your awareness to the gifts and strengths and potentialities in this being.... Behind those eyes are unmeasured reserves of courage and intelligence... of patience, endurance, wit and wisdom.... There are gifts there, of which this person her/himself is unaware.... Consider what these powers could do for the healing of our planet, if they were believed and acted on.... As you consider that, let yourself become aware of your desire that this person be free from fear, free from greed, released from hatred and from sorrow and from the causes of suffering. Know that what you are now experiencing is the great loving-kindness... .

Now as you look into those eyes, let yourself become aware of the pain that is there. There are sorrows accumulated in that life, as in all human lives, though you can only guess at them. There are disappointments and failures and losses and loneliness and abuse... there are hurts beyond the telling.... Let yourself open to that pain, to hurts that this person may never have told another being.... You cannot fix that pain but you can be with it. As you let yourself simply be with that suffering, know what you are experiencing is the great compassion. It is very good for the healing of our world.

---

1. Reprinted from *World As Lover, World As Self* (1991) by Joanna Macy with permission of Parallax Press, Berkeley, California.

As you look into the eyes of this person, consider how good it would be to work together...on a joint project, toward a common goal....What it could be like, taking risks together...conspiring together in zest and laughter...celebrating the successes, consoling each other over the setbacks, forgiving each other when you make mistakes...and simply being there for each other....As you open to that possibility, what you open to is the great wealth: the pleasure in each other's power, the joy in each other's joy.

Lastly, let your awareness drop deep within you like a stone, sinking below the level of what words can express, to the deep web of relationship that underlies all experience. It is the web of life in which you have taken being, in which you are supported, and that interweaves us through all space and time....See the being before you as if seeing the face of one who, at another time, another place, was your lover or your enemy, your parent or your child....And now you meet again on this brink of time....And you know your lives are as intricately interwoven as nerve cells in the mind of a great being....Out of that vast net you cannot fall...no stupidity, or failure, or cowardice, can ever sever you from that living web. For that is what you are....Rest in that knowing. Rest in the Great Peace....Out of it we can act, we can venture everything...and let every encounter be a homecoming to our true nature....Indeed it is so.

Facilitation

Once when I facilitated this exercise, two people who had never met were partners. At the end of the meditation, the woman asked the man, "Did your father die recently?"

The man was shocked. His father had died two weeks earlier. He asked her, "How could you possibly know?" She replied, "I saw it in your eyes."

This is a powerful exercise. The ability to see things from another person's perspective is a fundamental but largely dormant human capacity. During the discussion, help the group sort through their feelings and reactions. (You should not do this exercise if you have not done it yourself.) One of the first times I did this exercise as a participant, I became so self-conscious at times that I began to smirk and giggle. Be prepared. Some people may see no value in the exercise or may even become angry.

You need to help the group understand the business imperatives and broad implications of compassion. Ask them what role compassion plays in business. Why is it an important quality for a leader or manager? Putting aside the humanitarian aspects, compassion enables us to tune in to the needs and concerns of the people we work with and the customers we serve. Stories are a way of standing in another person's shoes, and of sharing our shoes with others.

Suggested Reading

Abrahams, Roger D. *African Folktales*. New York: Pantheon Books, 1983.

Armstrong, David M. *Managing by Storying Around: A New Method of Leadership*. New York: Doubleday, 1992.

Berman, Michael, and David Brown. *The Power of Metaphor*. New York: Crown House Publishing, 2001.

Boje, David. *Narrative Methods for Organizational & Communication Research*. London: Sage Publications, 2001.

Brown, John Seely, Stephen Denning, Katalina Groh, and Lawrence Prusak. *Storytelling in Organizations: Why Storytelling Is Transforming the 21st Century Organizations and Management*. Burlington, Mass: Elsevier Butterworth-Heinemann, 2005.

Brown, Juanita, and David Isaacs. *The World Café: Shaping Our Futures through Conversations that Matter*. San Francisco, Calif.: Berrett-Koehler, 2005.

Bushnaq, Inea. *Arab Folktales*. New York: Pantheon Books, 1986.

Calvino, Italo. *Italian Folktales*. New York: Harcourt Brace Jovanovich, 1980. Translated by George Martin and originally published in 1956 by Giulio Einaudi editore, s.p.a.

Campbell, Joseph. *The Power of Myth with Bill Moyers*. New York: Doubleday, 1988.

Canfield, Jack, and Jacqueline Miller. *Heart at Work: Stories and Strategies for Building Self-Esteem and Reawakening the Soul at Work*. New York: McGraw-Hill, 1996.

Chinen, Allan B. *In the Ever After: Fairy Tales and the Second Half of Life*. Wilmette, Ill.: Chiron, 1989.

Chinen, Allan B. *Once Upon a Midlife: Classic Stories and Mythic Tales To Illuminate the Middle Years.* New York: Tarcher/Putnam, 1992.

Clark, Evelyn. *Around the Corporate Campfire: How Great Leaders Use Stories To Inspire Success.* Sevierville, Tenn.: Insight, 2004.

Collins, R., and P. J. Cooper. *The Power of Story: Teaching through Storytelling.* Boston: Allyn & Bacon, 1996.

Creighton, Helen. *A Folk Tale Journey.* Wreck Cove, Cape Breton Island: Breton Books, 1993.

Denning, Stephen. *A Leader's Guide to Storytelling.* San Francisco: Jossey-Bass, 2005.

Denning, Stephen. *The Springboard: How Storytelling Ignites Action in Knowledge Era Organizations.* Boston: Butterworth-Heineman, 2001.

Denning, Stephen. *Squirrel Inc.: A Fable of Leadership through Storytelling.* San Francisco: Jossey-Bass, 2004.

Dorson, Richard M. *Folk Legends of Japan.* Rutland, Vt.: Charles E. Tuttle, 1962.

Erdoes, Richard, and Alfonso Ortiz. *American Indian Myths and Legends.* New York: Pantheon Books, 1984.

Feinstein, David, and Stanley Krippner. *The Mythic Path.* New York: Tarcher/Putnam, 1997.

Fulford, Robert. *The Triumph of Narrative: Storytelling in the Age of Mass Culture.* New York: Broadway, 2001.

Gabriel, Yiannis. *Storytelling in Organizations: Facts, Fictions, and Fantasies.* London: Oxford University Press, 2000.

Gardner, Howard, *Leading Minds: An Anatomy of Leadership.* New York: Basic Books, 1996.

Gargiulo, Terrence L. *Making Stories: A Practical Guide for Organizational Leaders and Human Resource Specialists.* Westport, Conn.: Greenwood Press, 2002.

Gargiulo, Terrence L. *The Strategic Use of Stories in Organizational Communication and Learning.* Armonk, N.Y.: M. E. Sharpe, 2005.

Garvin, David A. *Learning in Action: A Guide to Putting The Learning Organization To Work.* Boston: Harvard Business School Press, 2000.

Jensen, Bill. *Simplicty: The New Competitive Advantage in a World of More, Better, Faster.* Cambridge, Mass.: Perseus Books, 2000.

Lipman, Doug. *Improving Your Storytelling: Beyond the Basics for All Who Tell Stories in Work or Play.* Little Rock, Ark.: August House: 1999.

Maguire, Jack. *The Power of Personal Storytelling: Spinning Tales To Connect with Others.* New York: Tarcher/Putnam, 1998.

Meade, Erica Helm. *Tell It By Heart: Women and the Healing Power of Story.* Chicago: Open Court, 1995.

Moore, Thomas. *Dark Nights of the Soul: A Guide to Finding Your Way through Life's Ordeals.* New York: Gotham Books, 2004.

Morgan, Gareth. *Imaginization: New Mindsets for Seeing, Organizing, and Managing.* Thousand Oaks, Calif.: Sage, 1993.

Neuhauser, Peg C. *Corporate Legends and Lore: The Power of Storytelling as a Management Tool.* New York: McGraw-Hill Trade, 1993.

Norgaard, Mette. *The Ugly Duckling Goes to Work.* New York: AMACOM, 2005.

Owens, H. *Open Space Technology: A User's Guide.* San Francisco: Berrett-Koehler, 1997.

Parkin, Margaret. *Tales for Change: Using Storytelling To Develop People and Management.* London: Kogan Page, 2004.

Parkin, Margaret. *Tales for Coaching: Using Stories and Metaphors with Individuals & Small Groups.* London: Kogan Page, 2001.

Parkin, Margaret. *Tales for Trainers: Using Stories and Metaphors To Facilitate Learning.* London: Kogan Page, 1998.

Sawyer, Ruth. *The Way of the Storyteller.* New York: Penguin Books, 1976.

Schank, Roger. *Tell Me a Story: A New Look at Real and Artificial Memory.* Evanston, Ill.: Northwestern University Press, 1995.

Schank, Roger. *Virtual Learning: A Revolutionary Approach to Building a Highly Skilled Workforce.* New York: McGraw-Hill, 1997.

Senge, P. *The Fifth Discipline.* New York: Doubleday Books, 1990.

Simons, Annette. *The Story Factor.* Cambridge, Mass.: Perseus Publishing, 2001.

Stone, Richard. *The Healing Art of Storytelling: A Sacred Journey of Personal Discovery.* New York: Hyperion, 1996.

Tichy, Noel M., with Eli Cohen. *The Leadership Engine: How Winning Companies Build Leaders at Every Level.* New York: HarperCollins, 1997.

Wacker, Mary B., and Lori L. Silverman. *Stories Trainers Tell: 55 Ready-To-Use Stories To Make Training Stick.* San Francisco: Jossey-Bass/Pfeifffer, 2003.

Wendover, Robert, and Terrence Gargiulo. *On Cloud Nine: Weathering Generational Challenges in the Workplace.* New York: AMACOM, 2005.

Wheatley, Margaret J., and Myron Kellner-Rogers. *A Simpler Way.* San Francisco: Berrett-Koehler, 1996.

Wolkstein, Diane. *The Magic Orange Tree and Other Haitian Folktales.* New York: Schocken Books, 1978.

Zeitlin, Steve. *Because God Loves Stories: An Anthology of Jewish Storytelling.* New York: Touchstone, 1997.

Index

ABOUT THE AUTHOR

TERRENCE L. GARGIULO is an international speaker, author, organizational development consultant, and group process facilitator. He is a four-time author, and his first book has been translated into Chinese. He holds a Master of Management in Human Services from the Florence Heller School at Brandeis University and is a recipient of *Inc.* magazine's Marketing Master. Among his numerous clients, past and present, are General Motors, Dreyer's Ice Cream, DTE Energy, U.S. Coast Guard, Merck, Boston University, City of Boston, City of Lowell (Massachusetts), Arthur D. Little, Raytheon, and Coca-Cola. Terrence is a frequent presenter at conferences of the International Society of Performance Improvement, the American Society for Training and Development, and the Academy of Management.

For more information about consulting or leadership development retreats at the Environment for Organizational Improvement, contact:

Terrence Gargiulo   Telephone: 781-894-4381
121 Las Brisas Drive   E-mail: terrence@makingstories.net
Monterey, CA 93940   Web: http://www.makingstories.net